£2.90?

First published by James Brodie Ltd
This revised edition first published 1990
by Pan Books Ltd

Published 1994 by
THE MACMILLAN PRESS LTD
Houndmills, Basingstoke, Hampshire RG21 2XS
and London
Companies and representatives
throughout the world

ISBN 0–333–58139–3

Printed in Great Britain by
Cox and Wyman Ltd
Reading, Berkshire

Page references in these Notes are to the Penguin
edition of *Sons and Lovers*, but references are
also given to Parts and Chapters, so that
the Notes may be used with any edition of the novel.

Preface

The intention throughout this study aid is to stimulate and guide, to encourage your involvement in the book, and to develop informed responses and a sure understanding of the main details.

Brodie's Notes provide a clear outline of the play or novel's plot, followed by act, scene, or chapter summaries and/or commentaries. These are designed to emphasize the most important literary and factual details. Poems, stories or non-fiction texts combine brief summary with critical commentary on individual aspects or common features of the genre being examined. Textual notes define what is difficult or obscure and emphasize literary qualities. Revision questions are set at appropriate points to test your ability to appreciate the prescribed book and to write accurately and relevantly about it.

In addition, each of these Notes includes a critical appreciation of the author's art. This covers such major elements as characterization, style, structure, setting and themes. Poems are examined technically – rhyme, rhythm, for instance. In fact, any important aspect of the prescribed work will be evaluated. The aim is to send you back to the text you are studying.

Each study aid concludes with a series of general questions which require a detailed knowledge of the book: some of these questions may invite comparison with other books, some will be suitable for coursework exercises, and some could be adapted to work you are doing on another book or books. Each study aid has been adapted to meet the needs of the current examination requirements. They provide a basic, individual and imaginative response to the work being studied, and it is hoped that they will stimulate you to acquire disciplined reading habits and critical fluency.

Graham Handley 1990

Contents

The author and his work

David Herbert Lawrence was born at Eastwood, Nottinghamshire, 1885. He was the youngest in a family of four; his father was a miner who had worked in the pits from the age of seven, and his mother, the Mrs Morel of *Sons and Lovers*, came from a middle-class family in Nottingham. The boy's health was suspect from the start, and he could not become a collier; at the age of thirteen Lawrence won a scholarship to Nottingham High School, and later took a job as a clerk. He left this post in order to train as a teacher. After two years at Nottingham University College Lawrence was placed first in the All England and Wales Uncertificated Teachers' Examination. His first novel *The White Peacock* (1911), was published while he was teaching in Croydon.

By now Lawrence was writing poems and stories regularly, and he saw his future clearly as a professional writer. His mother, to whom he was devoted, had died in 1910, and some eighteen months after her death he met and fell in love with Frieda Weekley. She was a member of the distinguished German Von Richtofen family, and was married at the time of her meeting with D. H. Lawrence to Ernest Weekley, a professor at Nottingham University College. In 1912 she and Lawrence went to Germany together and in 1914, after her divorce from Weekley, they were married.

The war years saw them in England, and for a time in Cornwall, where Frieda was suspected of being a spy. Lawrence, who loathed the Germans and the Allies equally, was unfit for military service. In 1919 the Lawrences left England and travelled extensively, first in Europe (they visited Frieda's family) and then in Australia and America. A considerable period of their life together was spent in New Mexico on a ranch which was given to them by a sympathizer. Throughout these years of travel and temporary settlement, Lawrence was a prolific writer of poems, stories and novels, as well as on a variety of subjects from criticism and travel to history – whatever took his interest. The Lawrences returned to Europe in 1929; for some time the condition of his lungs had given cause for concern, and he finally died of tuberculosis in Vence, near Nice, on 2 March 1930.

In an excellent paper on Lawrence (*The Pelican Guide to English Literature, 7, The Modern Age*, pp.280–300) W. W. Robson, before analysing *Women in Love*, highlights the difficulties in giving a balanced view of D. H. Lawrence. It is sufficient to say that the skeleton career drawn above had its life in the flesh and blood of inspiration; but when that is said one is faced with a mass of literature – anecdotal, critical, defamatory, laudatory – beneath which the real D. H. Lawrence, man and artist, lies interred.

Shortly after his death Catherine Carswell published *The Savage Pilgrimage* (1932), a sympathetic account of Lawrence's life as she knew it, based on her friendship with him. The previous year the writer John Middleton Murry published his account, largely unsympathetic, in *Son of Woman, the story of D. H. Lawrence*; Murry's knowledge was based on the period in Cornwall during which he, Katherine Mansfield and the Lawrences had lived together. So it was in Lawrence's lifetime; he was the centre of controversy, sometimes deliberately self-engineered, sometimes as a result of misunderstanding or malice. *The Rainbow* (1915) was banned for obscenity, as was *Lady Chatterley's Lover* (1928), and it was not until the unexpurgated text of the latter was rescued from oblivion and exposed to the glare of notoriety incident upon a court case (1960) that Lawrence may be said to have been freed from the bondage which held him in life.

It is not the purpose of this section to look closely at any of Lawrence's individual works, but to indicate the general nature of his achievement and inspiration, in so far as anything concerning Lawrence can be dealt with in general rather than individual terms. If the student picks up novels as different in basis and execution as *The Plumed Serpent* and *Lady Chatterley's Lover*, he will be aware at once that this is no ordinary, conventional novelist operating in the mainstream of the traditional English novel.

Lawrence's writing is like no one else's; yet *Sons and Lovers*, for example, is a novel of provincial life, and has certain affinities with, say, *The Return of the Native* and *Middlemarch*. The differences, however, are much greater than the similarities. Perhaps the key to the differences lies in something that Lawrence wrote in the same year as the publication of *Sons and Lovers* to Ernest Collings. In this letter he speaks of his religion as being a belief in the blood and flesh as distinct from the intellect, stressing that we can err in our minds, but that the way our blood reacts, what it tells us to do and believe, is the truth. Consequently Lawrence has little time for knowledge as such, and refers to the intellect as a 'bit and a bridle'. He speaks of wanting an answer to his blood without the intervention 'of mind, or moral, or whatnot'. He sees man's body as a kind of flame, like a candle, always upright, always flowing, with the intellect as the light that is shed on things around. Lawrence is not concerned with the things around, but 'with the mystery of the flame forever flowing'.

This mystery was to be explored again and again, but what it means in practice is that Lawrence brought to his novels and stories a new, vivid, awareness of the primary things in life, felt and experienced rather than recorded for the reader's edification. A close study of *Mansfield Park*, a novel which exposes ironically and satirically some of the many frailties of human nature, reveals that, authorial commentary apart, we are given a very one-sided and limited view of the people who play the leading roles. The word 'play' has been used deliberately, for the characters are seen only when they are, so to speak, in the public view. We are told their thoughts, but we never touch the tingling fibres of their instinct.

Another example may be taken from an author Lawrence admired, George Eliot. When, in *Adam Bede*, the hero confronts Arthur Donnithorne, the seducer of Hetty Sorrel, and fells him with a blow which is finally delivered more in sadness than in anger, we know nothing of Adam's deepest state of emotion. But when Baxter and Paul fight in *Sons and Lovers* the primitive impulses of the unconscious are revealed. Paul acts without recourse to convention, education, upbringing; the result is a dimension of experience unplumbed before.

Lawrence would be the last to want us to use the now hackneyed terms to describe experiments in the English novel from Dorothy Richardson and Joyce in this century; terms like 'interior vision' and 'stream of consciousness' can have no direct reference to Lawrence, who trusted his instinct, so that his artistry is more intuitive than anything else in his early novels and stories, and this despite much rewriting.

Since Lawrence deals with the subconscious, the instinct, it is not surprising that much of his fiction focuses on one of the primary impulses of man, the sexual impulse. From the first to the last in Lawrence sexual awareness is pre-eminent; in elevating the driving force, and giving to its consummation something of the sublime, Lawrence not only wrote from his heart, but gave to the generations of writers who succeeded him a freedom which has, alas, been notoriously abused.

Those who pointed a finger accusingly at *Lady Chatterley's Lover* must have forgotten the sexuality of, for example, *Hamlet*; they cannot have read Chaucer, Fielding, Balzac or Maupassant. Yet even where Lawrence feels the most strongly, he is at times contradictory in attitude. Paul and Clara fall from the pinnacle of consummation, and the same happens to Ursula and Skrebensky in *The Rainbow*. It is never stated overtly, but one has the impression that sexual fulfilment cannot be sustained without an accompanying spiritual fulfilment. In *The Rainbow* it seems that the woman must not submit, but must retain her individuality, her essential being; in *The Plumed Serpent* the woman's physical fulfilment is dependent upon her acceptance of the guiding authority of the man. None the less, some of the most beautiful lyrical passages in Lawrence's writings exalt the sexual act without any of the overtones or innuendo which denigrate it in so much of our contemporary fiction and drama.

It is not the place here to discuss in any detail Lawrence's writings which do not reflect in some way on *Sons and Lovers*. The latter, for example, is not didactic, it does not contain a message which the author insists on hammering into the reader's consciousness, though much of Lawrence's writing has strains of prophecy (*Fantasia of the Unconscious*, for example). What it does contain is that element of poetry which is found in all his writings and that quality of painting which he and Paul Morel possessed.

Lawrence's poetry is of a very high order and, once again, he is indebted to nobody. R. A. Scott-James in *Fifty Years of English Literature* discovers a likeness to Swinburne in certain cadences and verse forms that Lawrence uses (he also describes Swinburne as a forerunner of Lawrence in uncovering the deepest sexual impulses), but Swinburne never once saw nature as Lawrence knew her. In the novels and stories there is frequently a symbolic or mystical association with natural description, as in Mrs Morel's experience with the lilies when she is shut out by Morel in *Sons and Lovers*, or the reiterative mention of chrysanthemums in *Odour of Chrysanthemums*. Some of Lawrence's poetry, like some of the passages in his novels, is a passing, intensely vivid impression picked up at a moment in time and used later.

Another technique, common to Lawrence's prose and poetry, is the constant emphasis of a colour, a sound, an impression, by the use of multiple repetition. The effect is never diminished, always enhanced and, as in the poetry, there is often a rhythmic accompaniment which registers on the consciousness of the reader.

Another aspect of Lawrence's work which must be mentioned in any consideration of his life is his mastery of that underrated form, the short story. Some of Lawrence's stories are in fact long, equivalent to the German *novelle*, like *The Man Who Died* and *St Mawr*. Some are genuine short stories, like *The Odour of Chrysanthemums* and *Jimmy and the Desperate Woman*. In any of the novels, it will be noticed that some of the episodes are stories in themselves; the first chapter of *Sons and Lovers* is just such a story. Since Lawrence saw things in a new way, and set them down in a new way, very frequently the small canvas gave him the right dimension for an impression recollected more in excitement than in tranquillity. The result is that the miner's death, obvious and awaited, in *Odour of Chrysanthemums*, never fails to provoke the reader's attention. That sense of incompleteness in the human relation which comes with the knowledge of death is here given an entirely new direction; for the wife looking at her dead husband realizes what a mockery their intimacy has been since she has no knowledge of the man who now lies before her, and to whom she has been married for so long. This is perhaps part 'of the mystery of the flame forever flowing' previously referred to.

It is this intense individuality which gives to the work of D. H. Lawrence a transcendent value. That he has limitations it would be foolish to deny. Some of his work is over-written, exhibiting not so much a belief in one's instinct as a demonstration of the ingenuity of the human mind; complex people are made to act and feel in complex ways in fundamentally simple situations. Sometimes Lawrence's style is slipshod, giving the impression of hastiness in composition, or it is conversational, with vivid metaphors alongside slangy platitudes, as in *The Virgin and the Gypsy*. Lawrence unquestionably breathed life into the English novel, wrote many stories of arresting interest and lasting worth and much poetry which, set in its time, is way ahead of that time in form and content.

He has been called a restless and unhappy man, and if one remembers Lawrence's health – he was badly ill with chest trouble while teaching at Croydon – and the constant tension he suffered over the publication of his works, the war and, initially, his marriage, it is hardly surprising that one pictures a man worn from without and within by driving passions, some of which were satisfied by his writing, his wife or his travelling life. But if the student reads some of Lawrence's early letters he will realize how close to common everyday humanity he was, and how free from anger and affectation he was in some respects as a young man. In such letters Lawrence reveals his sense of insecurity, a strong core of loyalty to family and friends, a love of children and an impetuosity of action which are endearing in their simplicity, though in later life they were to become tortuous and tortured.

Lawrence writes, too, of his work, telling Edward Garnett of his 'immortal Heinemann novel, *Paul Morel*', and he displays a detailed knowledge of English fiction, both contemporary and traditional; Lawrence's mind, as well as his instinct, told him how to shape his own novels and stories. There is some emotional over-praising and blaming in *The Collected Letters*, together with some astute comments which give a valuable insight into his own feelings. For example, he tells Rachel Jennings to 'Read *Anna Karenina* – no matter, read it again, and if you dare to fall out with it, I'll – I'll swear aloud', and to Jessie Chambers, 'I often think Stendhal must have writhed in torture every time he remembered *Le Rouge et Le Noir* was public property'.

Lawrence read widely and deeply – witness his comments on *Oedipus*, *The Trojan Women* and *The Bacchae* – but he wrote with superb independence and directness. There are more complete novelists than Lawrence, novelists who have paid perhaps greater attention to form and structure, or who have observed scrupulously the canons of their craft. It is typical of Lawrence's outlook that when *The Rainbow* was banned in 1915 he asked that Henry James should read it and give his opinion as to whether it merited banning or not; yet no two novelists could be farther apart in aim and practice than Lawrence and James.

Lawrence is no great delineator of manners, conventions, sentiment, romance, or even the social life of his own time, which so many writers take as their natural material; but in the impulses and instincts of interacting people, in intimate conscious or unconscious contention or consummation, he is unsurpassed in his real and vibrant identification. And if one adds to this a power of observation which sees Nature as she is, simply, or symbolically in relation to his characters, then Lawrence is perhaps the greatest novelist of this century, and one of the most meaningful for our own time. Lawrence lived, and his writing is 'the precious life-blood' of, at least, a major creative artist.

Source and theme

Source

Sons and Lovers is an autobiographical account of Lawrence's early life. The novel was originally called *Paul Morel*, and its development can be followed by studying Lawrence's correspondence between 1910 and 1913. In a letter to Rachel Annand Taylor which was written six days before the death of his mother, Lawrence gives an account of his mother which shows how strongly she influenced the conception of *Sons and Lovers*. In it he writes of her as being a clever and ironical woman of good old burgher descent who married beneath herself. During the course of their marriage Lawrence's father revealed a lack of principle, deceived his wife, lied to her, and drank. The result was that Mrs Lawrence showed contempt for her husband, and, realizing this, he continued to drink. Lawrence describes the friction between them, and refers to his own hatred of his father; he even shivered with horror when his father touched him.

There grew up between mother and son a bond, so that they 'loved each other, almost with a husband and wife love' as well as with the natural affection of mother and son. His mother once told his aunt that he (Lawrence) was part of her, and Lawrence says with terrible self-honesty that they knew each by instinct, and that so strong was the knowledge that it made him in some respects 'abnormal'. At the time of writing Lawrence believed that such an intense fusion of soul could not come twice in a lifetime, and adds 'Now my mother is nearly dead, and I don't quite know how I am'.

Obviously in any novel which has an autobiographical framework there is some fiction, but the following identifications can safely be made: Paul Morel – D. H. Lawrence; Mrs Morel – Lydia Beardsall Lawrence, his mother, who died of cancer on 9 December 1910. Walter Morel – Lawrence's father Arthur John Lawrence, who lived until 1924. William Morel – his elder brother William, who died in 1901. Annie Morel – Lawrence's sister Ada, who married Edward Clarke in 1913, and lived until

1948. Miriam Leivers – Jessie Chambers, later Wood, who has left her own account of her relationship with Lawrence in *D. H. Lawrence: A Personal Record* 1935. Clara Dawes – Alice Dax, wife of Harry Dax, an Eastwood pharmacist. She was a feminist and a suffragette.

In a letter to Edward Garnett, written in 1912, Lawrence writes of the main outlines of the plot and the characters in such a way as to show how much of his home life had been absorbed and reshaped by the creative impulse. He tells of how a woman of principle and breeding steps down into a working-class world and has little satisfaction in her own life. Physically drawn to her husband, she gives birth to children who reflect their parents' passion for one another in their own vitality. But as her sons mature, she singles out first the eldest, then the next, as lovers, and pushes them out into life by the sheer force of her love.

However, when they become men they cannot love in the full sense of the term, for their mother has been the dominating influence in their life and still continues to hold them. When they come into contact with women, the disruption of their lives is apparent. William makes love to a superficial and silly young woman, but his mother retains her grip on his soul. The split kills him because he is so bewildered. The next son meets a girl who fights for possession of his soul. This son, like the others, loves his mother and hates his father, and the battle goes on between the girl and the mother for possession. Gradually the mother proves the stronger and the son decides – like his brother before him – to yield up his soul and settle for sexual love. This he gets, the sense of disruption comes over him, but the mother, feeling this sense in her son, begins to die. The son gives up his mistress, nurses his dying mother and in the end is left without anything; the final implication is of a drift towards death.

Comment on this would only be superfluous. Think of the two accounts, try to estimate their difference of mood, and it will be seen how the artist works on his own emotions and reactions, in this case translating deeply experienced feelings into a moving human record.

Background and plot

Background

The background to the novel is life in the mining village of Bestwood (Eastwood) in Nottinghamshire, and the period covered is the first twenty-five years of the life of Paul Morel (D. H. Lawrence), roughly 1885–1910, the date of Mrs Morel's (Lawrence's mother's) death. We witness the struggle of a mother to prevent her children from being sucked into the mining village community, in which the men and the women have clearly differentiated functions in life. Mrs Morel's fears can be shown by the clear split between pit and 'pub' and home. The evils of this society are impressed upon the reader: the pit; the tight-knit community of the street; the gossip and the extra work undertaken by the women; the man coming home to his meal and expecting it to be ready, etc.

Mrs Morel belongs to the local women's guild – 'the "clat-fart" shop' – and these references are part of the novel's concern with the position of women in a male dominated society. They extend throughout the novel – Mrs Morel prepares her papers for the guild, Clara is a suffragette addressing women's meetings, Miriam is a sensitive and spiritual girl humiliated by the practical family men.

By the time we meet Miriam and Clara, however, we are moving beyond Bestwood. Willey Farm, Miriam's home, epitomizes healthy, outdoor work; good, animal activity which makes Paul a rather more robust character than hitherto. It also provides a contrast with the urban society of Bestwood and with Paul's work at Thomas Jordan's; the beauty of the countryside is investigated sometimes in lyrical detail. It provides the backdrop for Miriam's mysticism and possessiveness, and for Paul's frustration and wonderment. Descriptions of nature provide an atmospheric background, a symbol, perhaps, of his characters' experiences.

There is also the Nottingham background: Jordan's, which witnesses his affair with Clara; the street where Clara lives, and of which she is so ashamed; the cathedral and, very significantly, the river, which symbolizes their passion. The city is used as a background to the affair of Paul and Clara, but it is never a presence in the novel. The real backgrounds are the Morel household, the mining village community, Willey Farm and nature and, most poignantly, the Morel household again as Mrs Morel lies dying.

Plot

Sons and Lovers is an exposition of the lives of the Morel family: set towards the end of the last century, the action takes us into the early years of this. The interaction of Mr and Mrs Morel is described, together with the upbringing of the four Morel children. A retrospective sequence tells how Gertrude Coppard married Walter Morel, and stresses the disillusion which she experiences as a result of her discovery that Morel has misled her about the rent of the house and the purchase of the furniture. The pattern of the marriage after the first six months or so is outlined; Morel drinks regularly, often keeping his wife short of essential housekeeping money, and when he is drunk he is sometimes violent.

Mrs Morel abhors drink and, despite periods when Morel is a warm-hearted and good father, the children despise him because of his treatment of their mother. Mrs Morel is ambitious for her sons, and lives for them and their successful futures. William, the eldest, does very well at school and gets a job with a shipping firm in London. Paul, the second son, obtains a position with a surgical appliance manufacturer in Nottingham.

Mrs Morel seems well on the way to seeing her ambitions realized, when William becomes enamoured of a socially pretentious girl. He brings her home to visit the family, and reveals that his engagement is causing him more worry than happiness. After one visit home he returns to London; shortly afterwards a telegram arrives announcing that he is ill. She goes at once, but William dies, of pneumonia, in a terrible paroxysm. The shadow of this death casts itself long over the family: Paul, neglected because of his mother's absorption in William's death, also contracts pneumonia. He is nursed by his mother and recovers.

While Paul is convalescing his mother takes him to see some friends of hers, the Leivers, who live at Willey Farm. The young man becomes very friendly with the highly spiritual, impractical daughter of the house, Miriam, and enjoys the family atmosphere; for the next few years this becomes a second home. Paul's friendship with Miriam deepens into an intimate relationship, though on his side the feeling cannot be strictly defined as one of love, for her possessiveness plus her incapacity for physical demonstration and general uncertainty militates against Paul's giving of himself. Mrs Morel and most of Paul's friends dislike Miriam. She, however, while realizing this, is reasonably content; but Paul comes to believe that the spiritual aspect of love by itself is not enough for him.

Later Miriam introduces him to a friend of hers, Clara Dawes, a firm believer in women's rights, who is separated from her husband. They eventually become lovers. Paul has already decided to break with Miriam, a decision which is strengthened when he discovers that his mother is ill. Meanwhile, the other Morel children are settling. Annie marries her dependable Leonard and moves to Sheffield; Arthur, in a moment of impetuosity, joins the army, but later marries Beatrice Wyld, leaves the army for a steady job, and succumbs to domestic life.

As Paul becomes more intimate with Clara, his mother's illness worsens. One night Paul is attacked by Clara's husband: he is nursed back to strength again by his mother, and takes a short holiday. On his return he visits Annie in Sheffield and finds that Mrs Morel is there, very ill indeed. Paul gets a specialist to see her, she is taken home to Bestwood, and there follows the long description of her gradual death: eventually Paul and Annie give her an overdose of morphia. Paul is left, at the end, 'derelict'. He has already brought Baxter and Clara together again; he seeks out Miriam, but soon realizes that his future does not lie with her. He hovers between the wish to join his mother in death and the desire to go on living. The last words of the novel perhaps reflect his determination to keep a hold on life whatever the cost.

Structure and style

Structure

In the ideal sense of the term, which implies that there is a complete entity of form to which everything in the novel subscribes, *Sons and Lovers* is structurally uneven, and there are episodes which could be safely omitted without loss to the overall effect. But Lawrence tends to have a structural flair, so that the novel falls naturally and easily into sections. The divisions in Part 1 are as follows:

1 The description of the Morel family and its domestic disharmony brought about by the drinking of the father.

2 This leads us to the focus being squarely on Mrs Morel, Paul and William.

3 In turn this prepares the way for the death of William and the family reaction, with a sharper focus on Paul when he becomes seriously ill.

Part 2, which covers the life of Paul from the late teens to the mid-twenties, is concerned exclusively with him until the serious illness and subsequent death of Mrs Morel. Everything is seen through Paul's eyes; this is a contrast with the first three chapters of Part 1, in which Mrs Morel was the acknowledged standpoint from which most incidents were viewed. The divisions in Part 2 are as follows:

1 Paul, in late adolescence, falls spiritually in love with Miriam Leivers.

2 He later rejects Miriam because of his mother's illness and also because of his feeling for Clara Dawes, Miriam's friend, a suffragette who is separated from her husband.

3 Describes the gradual ripening of Paul's physical passion for Clara, her response to it, and their coming together.

4 Paul, beaten up by Baxter Dawes, is nursed by his mother and grows away from Clara.

5 Mrs Morel's illness, leading to her death, and also to Paul's realization that he cannot give himself fully to a woman while his mother lives, as a result of which he brings about a reconciliation between Clara and Baxter.

6 The effect of Mrs Morel's death on Paul, his re-meeting Miriam, and his apparent will to carry on after the initial temptation of suicide.

The chapter headings are clear signposts to the road the novel is taking. Generally each one indicates the main bias of the chapter, but inevitably material not covered by the suggestion of the title is included. The open ending gives the novel firmness, at the same time completing the naturalness which has been its main characteristic throughout. Whether it is instinct or art, the parts of the novel cohere just as the various parts of our lives cohere, and the formative flow of existence gives *Sons and Lovers* a structural unity which is never artificial or arbitrary.

Style

Lawrence's writing is strongly individualized, seeming to owe little or nothing to the traditional English novelists. In *Sons and Lovers* style is mood, whether it be the lyrical contemplation of nature or the reflexes of emotion in Paul as he longs for Clara. Like all great writers Lawrence uses a variety of styles, each appropriate to the character or situation he is describing.

One of the salient characteristics of Lawrence's style is his use of repetition, and this characteristic is markedly present in all his work. He will repeat a word or a phrase, often rhythmically as in a poem, in order to fix it in the reader's consciousness, and to bring about a certain response; he also uses the casual repetitions of conversation, which people inadvertently employ. A good example of the latter is where Mrs Morel, telling the children of their father's accident, uses the phrase 'of course' three times in a short paragraph (Chapter 5, p.109). There is, too, a form of repetition, not so much of phrase as of association, which is employed in the descriptions of Miriam, where religious images – for example, her eyes 'were usually dark as a dark church' (Chapter 7, p.190) – form a connected sequence and move from the simplicity of the one quoted here to terms like baptism, communion, ecstasy, 'one of the women who went with

Mary when Jesus was dead' (7,191). All these contribute to the quintessential spirituality of Miriam.

Lawrence's images – vivid, sudden metaphors and similes – give a sharpness and immediacy to his writing and occasionally, as above, a running irony. He uses natural comparisons from his age – sometimes from industry or the pit which was the background to his home life – and telling, economical commonplaces, as when he describes Pappleworth's terrier as being 'so like a wet rag that would never dry' (5,138). But the most exquisite images involve nature, as in 'the bluebells stood in pools of azure, under the new green hazels, upon a pale fawn floor of oak leaves' (6,155), and 'blue as a jay-bird's feather' (6,162).

Lawrence frequently uses personification in an unstilted and unobtrusive way, and probably the best example of this is the individuality he gives to the ash-tree which stands outside the house to which the Morels move. The ash-tree is a symbol of mood. Thus when Mr and Mrs Morel are quarrelling there is a 'piercing medley of shrieks and cries from the great, windswept ash-tree' (4,78); but when Paul, in his new-found security at Jordan's, returns home after the first week with his wages, we are told that the 'ash-tree seemed a friend now' (5,141). This is a subtle way of indicating how changed circumstances cause us to view familiar things in a new light.

Lawrence's irony is usually direct and obvious, as it is in the princess and the swinegirl references which surround Miriam; and by having the latter think of Mary Queen of Scots and Walter Scott heroines, Lawrence suggests that fantasy is more important to Miriam than life, and this underlines her incapacity for practical living. However, perhaps the most powerful instance of irony and symbol used conjointly in *Sons and Lovers* occurs when Paul, Miriam and Clara meet Miss Limb and the horse she loves so much (9,288–90). Every word Miss Limb utters reflects her isolation and frustration at not being able to love naturally; the horse is the symbol, the substitute, for the man she never has; and the scene stresses for Paul his own frustrations over Miriam, and for Clara her frustration, as yet unacknowledged, at rejecting normal life for feminist activity.

It has been said that *Sons and Lovers* style is mood, and this can be demonstrated by two or three instances which have a mystical content. The most obvious, perhaps, occurs in Chapter 1; Mrs

Morel, shut out in the garden by her husband, almost loses the sense of her own identity, and the atmosphere generated certainly partakes of the mystical:

The tall white lilies were reeling in the moonlight, and the air was charged with their perfume, as with a presence. Mrs Morel gasped slightly in fear. She touched the big, pallid flowers on their petals, then shivered. They seemed be stretching in the moonlight (1,35).

This is far from simple personification, yet integral to Lawrence's work, and we might set it beside Paul's contemplation of nature and the universe after his coming together with Clara, or Miriam's seeking out the bush which *she* possesses, and showing it to Paul.

Sons and Lovers is written in the third person, and occasionally the author interrupts the narrative to make a pronouncement. Thus when Mrs Morel is expecting Paul she has moments of bitterness over her powerlessness, and Lawrence observes: 'Sometimes life takes hold of one, carries the body along, accomplishes one's history, and yet is not real, but leaves oneself as it were slurred over' (1,13).

This is a convention of 19th-century fiction, where the omniscient author frequently controls the reader's responses, as Thackeray does, for example, in *Vanity Fair*. Lawrence interrupts rarely, and as Paul matures, not at all, for the third person narrator becomes submerged in the character whose life he is chronicling, and almost everything is seen through Paul's eyes. Like many of his 19th-century predecessors, and regional novelists of any period, Lawrence uses the dialect of the area he is describing. However, Lawrence goes a step further than Hardy or George Eliot, for example, by having his characters who have acquired standard speech relapse into dialect when the occasion demands. Morel himself is heard only in dialect throughout the novel, but it is thicker when he is moved to tenderness or anger; the courtship scene between Arthur and Beatrice is conducted in dialect, which somehow gives it an added intimacy, and when Paul has made love to Clara he is particularly tender to her, and uses dialect to convey his warmth. This dialect is convincing, full of proverbial twists and turns, and gives the setting of the novel and the characters in it a studied authenticity.

Much of the dialogue of the novel is in dialect but, whether

Lawrence is using this form of speech or the more sophisticated usage of the educated, the conversational exchanges of his characters have the ring of truth. We know and understand Paul and his mother as much by their speech as by the descriptions of them; Lawrence has a wonderful ear for tone and innuendo, and the language used by 'Gyp', Mr Pappleworth, Mr Jordan and Mrs Radford reveals succinctly the nature of their characters.

A close reading of *Sons and Lovers* will demonstrate Lawrence's familiarity with literature and, more particularly, with the Bible, which is constantly employed, sometimes ironically, to demonstrate a parallel with the life of one of his characters. Thus when Mr Heaton talks of the Wedding at Cana, Mrs Morel observes: 'Yes, poor fellow, his young wife is dead; that is why he makes his love into the Holy Ghost' (2,46).

Scattered throughout *Sons and Lovers* there are Biblical cadences which show just how great was the influence of the Bible upon Lawrence. Thus when Paul is nursed by his mother we are told that 'He put his head on her breast, and took ease of her for love' (6,175).

But perhaps Lawrence's style in the first and last instance is at its best in the mastery of mood. Consider the superb economy which conveys the shock and suddenness of anguish when Mrs Morel goes to London:

Mrs Morel settled down to nurse. She prayed for William, prayed that he would recognize her. But the young man's face grew more discoloured. In the night she struggled with him. He raved, and raved, and would not come to consciousness. At two o'clock, in a dreadful paroxysm, he died. (6,169)

Or consider the sentences which describe Paul's physical longing for Clara:

He went and got some dinner. All the time he was still under chloroform, and every minute was stretched out indefinitely. He walked miles of street. Then he thought he would be late at the meeting-place. He was at the Fountain at five past two. The torture of the next quarter of an hour was refined beyond expression. It was the anguish of combining the living self with the shell. Then he saw her. She came! And he was there. (12,372)

Here the short sentences indicate the emotional temperature of Paul, and his inability to settle at all until he has seen Clara. To read *Sons and Lovers* is to enjoy the poetry of expression and of the commonplaces of life. If Jane Austen and Henry James, to use two obvious examples, write in a formal, mannered way, then Lawrence writes on an informal level, with every now and then a brief word-picture, or an extended indulgence of colour, or an experience, or a sound, or any number of things which the consciousness turns into words without over-refinement. Lawrence's style smells of life rather than the lamp; the words *are* the experience.

Chapter summaries, critical commentary, textual notes and revision questions

Part I

Chapter 1 The Early Married Life of the Morels

The novel opens with some descriptions of 'Hell Row' and 'The Bottoms', two blocks of miners' cottages; Lawrence also gives an account of the mining history in the area. Mrs Morel is introduced at a particular time of her life – she is expecting her third child – and has recently moved to the family's new home in 'The Bottoms'. William, her eldest child, goes to the fair and, to his intense pride, his mother later puts in an appearance at the fair herself. We learn that Mr Morel, a miner, spends much of his time drinking and helping in the 'Moon and Stars', the local public-house. Mrs Morel broods on the unchanging pattern of her life. When her husband comes home late at night we can clearly see the differences between man and wife, and Lawrence further underlines this by taking us back into the past to show how they met and married.

For the first few months their married life together had been happy. Morel had 'signed the pledge', and had demonstrated what a handy man he was about the house, but Mrs Morel learns by chance that the furniture is unpaid for, and that the house is rented from her mother-in-law. She learns, too, that her husband drinks. With William's birth the real battle between husband and wife begins. Mrs Morel is protective, Mr Morel jealous of his son; Mrs Morel tries to make her husband meet his responsibilities, Mr Morel 'could not endure it – it drove him out of his mind'. On one occasion when William is about a year old, he cuts all his son's curls (his mother's pride) off, a demonstration which marks another step in their estrangement. The nature of Morel's work, plus his dislike for authority and his habits, lead to the family suffering temporary hardships, with Mrs Morel having to eke out her money to feed them.

After this deliberately sketchy review of the marriage, Lawrence brings us back to the day of the fair, when Morel's friend, Jerry Purdy, comes to call for him to go to Nottingham. The two men's day trip is described, followed by the return of Morel late at night, drunk. There is a terrible quarrel between husband and wife, and Mrs Morel is turned out into the garden by her husband. The latter falls into a drunken sleep, but later Mrs Morel succeeds in rousing him by tapping at the window. He gets up and lets her in.

gin-pits Shallow mines or pit-shafts worked by apparatus for hoisting, pumping etc., usually a drum or windlass worked by horse- or wind-power.

the few colliers and the donkeys . . . like ants A simile which at once indicates Lawrence's compassion for the miners and the beasts at their semingly endless toil.

stockingers People who work at stocking hand-looms, framework-knitters, stocking-weavers.

Lord Palmerston (1784–1865) British Foreign Secretary and Prime Minister, a dominating political figure during the early and middle Victorian period.

Carthusians An order of monks founded by St Bruno in 1086.

linked by a loop of fine chain, the railway A typically economical metaphor.

regiments of miners Note the irony of the term. Like soldiers, the miners have no freedom.

like the dots on a blank-six domino The image evokes the simple domestic pleasures of the miners, as well as being a vivid word-picture.

auriculas and saxifrage Primulas and rock plants.

dormer windows Projecting upright windows in a sloping roof.

nasty Lawrence often uses the colloquial (not specific) term which the people themselves might use.

a kind of aristocracy An appropriate term to define the fact that Mrs Morel is 'different', and it prepares us for the account of her past which establishes that she is a 'lady'.

be-out Without. Dialect and slang, sometimes a combination of both, are a commonplace in this novel.

the first small braying of a merry-go-round Notice that 'braying' has an onomatopoeic quality.

little stick Miserable, perverse child.

Aunt Sally man Refers to the game in which players throw sticks at a pipe in the mouth of a wooden woman's head. Probably a man standing behind a screen would add to the fun by making noises, pretending that he was hurt.

peep-show A small exhibition of pictures viewed through a lens in an opening.

'lowance i.e. payment in beer if not in money.

trough of darkness A vivid metaphor, imaginatively linked with the 'swilling' of her husband, and the drinking of other men who are now lurching down the road.

Sometimes life . . . as it were slurred over Lawrence rarely interrupts
the action of *Sons and Lovers*, but when he does the comment as here, is
weighted with his vision of life.

mended Dialect (Midlands) meaning 'made up'.

burgher Citizen, i.e. middle-class stock.

Colonel Hutchinson (1616–64) One of the Puritan leaders in the
English Revolution (1640–60); he signed the death warrant of the
King, but broke with Cromwell when the latter became all-powerful.

favoured i.e. resembled.

like a lace scarf Again a simile from domestic observation. A lace scarf
would probably be a best one.

comic grotesque He was a great mimic, and varied his tone of voice
humorously.

scallops Ornamental edging cut in material in imitation of the mollusc
shell, which is divided into radiating grooves and ridges.

She was still perfectly intact . . . full of beautiful candour She had her
full integrity and independence, and her forthright frankness was
beautiful to observe.

his face the flower of his body Note the superb economy of this
metaphor.

the Apostle Paul Trained to severity, he was converted to Christianity
and probably did more to promote belief in the Christian faith than
any of the other Apostles. Perhaps it is the association with her father,
and the fact that her third child is born in severity in the sense that her
married life has become 'severe', that causes Mrs Morel to call him
Paul.

Roger de Coverley A country dance and tune, the name derived from
Sir Roger de Coverley, the benevolent country squire immortalized by
Addison in the *Spectator*.

dusky, golden softness . . . gripped into incandescence A
characteristically lyrical note struck by Lawrence when he is dealing
with the physical appeal of one person for another.

taking the curl out of me i.e. taking my measure, discovering what I
am really like.

I'm like a pig's tail One of many examples which indicate Lawrence's
easy introduction of colloquial and proverbial phrases which give the
novel a solid basis of authenticity.

moudiwarp (Obviously the mole.) From mouldwarp, it can also mean a
mole-catcher.

pure humility Again the stress on the future Mrs Morel's integrity.

'ter You.

'Appen Perhaps.

He had signed the pledge, and wore the blue ribbon of a teetotaller
i.e. he had agreed to abstain from taking intoxicating drink. Non-
conformist sects encouraged such abstinence.

She saw him . . . but without understanding i.e. he listened to her
because she was a lady, but had no comprehension of what she said.

Tha s'lt ha'e You shall have.

frock-coat A man's long-skirted coat not cut away in the front.

carryin's-on Misbehaviour, usually in the moral sense of the word.

The woman dropped the clothes An expressive way of showing that Mrs Morel does not know what her husband does do.

There began . . . it drove him out of his mind Notice the superb economy with which a domestic situation which lasts a lifetime is described.

scathed him with her satire Mocked him viciously, cynically, with her tongue.

poll Top of the head.

a myriad of crescent-shaped curls . . . a marigold The vivid colour of the image heightens the contrast with the bareness of William's head.

But he felt something final had happened Note again the economy of the phrase.

She remembered the scene . . . suffered most intensely An early pointer to the overpoweringly possessive character of Mrs Morel.

the spear through the side One of the many Biblical echoes.

she wielded the lash i.e. of her tongue.

blab-mouthed An adjective which means 'talking too freely'.

gaffer The foreman of a gang.

clunch Soft white limestone.

niver fun Never found.

It'll 'appen carry thee ter bed an' back A sarcastic rejoinder – 'you know enough to last out the day and to keep going the next day'.

butty The colloquial meaning is 'mate', but in mining it generally means the middleman between the proprietor and the miners. Here it seems to refer to Morel.

stalls Working compartments in a mine.

'Sluther Slide, slip.

shonna Will not.

mucky little 'ussy Morel uses this either as a term of abuse or a term of endearment. Here it is the latter.

as if his head were on a wooden spring A simple image which conveys the buoyancy of a man when he is in a good mood.

conceived such a violent dislike of her husband . . . haemorrhage This presages Mrs Morel's own reactions to the presence of Morel when she is dying.

wizzen-hearted stick Mean, obstinate person.

opener-handed More generous.

dipping-hole A hollow in the meadow where water accumulated from the stream, thus forming a natural paddling-cum-bathing pool.

"Genevieve" A popular, sentimental song.

bezzle Drink hard.

The moon was high and magnificent . . . Then the presence of the night came again to her A colourful piece of writing in which the contrast of the cold outside and the violent heat within Mrs Morel as a result of her husband's treatment of her creates a living atmosphere.

The tall white lilies . . . as with a presence A mystical, poetic effect is achieved. Flowers are often used symbolically by Lawrence.

They seemed to be stretching . . . It almost made her dizzy This shows how Lawrence makes natural life a living background for human life. It is almost as if the lilies are coming into their own at night, and that somehow Mrs Morel in her suffering is linked to them. The next paragraph emphasizes this and carries the mystical experience one stage further.

ricocheted Notice how this sudden movement brings Mrs Morel back to herself. The word is arresting to the reader.

ruffles A minutely observant metaphor.

sound of a train like a sigh Note again the truth of the comparison.

chock A subtly onomatopoeic word.

bursten Split (rarely used in this form now).

For some time . . . snapping and jetting sparks Consider how appropriate the image is not only to Mrs Morel's mood but also to the pit/train images which are an integral part of Lawrence's writing.

Chapter 2 The Birth of Paul, and another Battle

This chapter opens with a description of Morel's penitence for his behaviour; his daily routine is described, and husband and wife are revealed in their commonplace exchanges by way of contrast with their embittered ones. After a short account of the stocking-making practice in The Bottoms, there follows the birth of Paul. The day for husband and wife – Mrs Morel in pain, her husband working savagely at the pit – reveals again how far apart they are emotionally and sympathetically. He is too tired to respond to her, she is too obstinate to respond to him. The result is emotional frustration for both.

Mrs Morel is visited by a congregational clergyman, Mr Heaton, and during one of these visits Morel returns from the pit. He is aggressive and coarse, shaming his wife before the refined and well-meaning young man who has no conception of what his life is like. There are often scenes in which Morel assaults his children, and after one of these Mrs Morel goes out with Annie and the baby. She focuses all her thoughts and emotions on the latter, and this is the beginning of that overwhelmingly possessive love which is to dominate his life and hers.

There follows a terrible scene when Morel returns drunk one night, startles the baby with his noise, and flings a drawer at his wife; her eye is cut, but she keeps her presence of mind, nurses the baby, and ministers to herself, though somewhat hindered by her drunken, albeit repentant, husband. Next morning Mrs Morel minimizes what has happened, telling her children (who do not believe her) that she has knocked herself against the latch of the coal-place. Morel's reaction is to stay in bed on the following two days until it is time to go to the public-house.

Morel cannot bring himself to approach her and apologize for his brutality. When he does appear he eats silently and alone, and the sense of misery pervades the house; when he goes to the 'Palmerston', he feels secure in the warmth of other men and forgets his responsibilities and misdoings. Later he steals sixpence from Mrs Morel's purse; when confronted with this he denies it, and collects a bundle of his belongings, saying that he will leave home. Of course he does not do so, and returns at night sulky and ashamed.

The only real rest . . . when he was out of the house This reflects how complete is the division between them from her point of view.

chemise A woman's undergarment.

no 'casions ter stir a peg No need for you to do much work today.

wagging on Keeping on, as a dog's tail keeps wagging.

copperful of clothes i.e. a full load of washing.

old-fashioned trap A cart on which the bundles were carried.

If you wouldn't mind That is, if you wouldn't mind coming in to help me.

loose-all The ending of the working shift.

Sorry Probably 'Sir' from 'Sirrah'.

Niver while the world stands Notice the exaggeration which echoes Morel's mood, and forms an effective contrast with what is happening to his wife at this moment.

hackin' thy guts out Straining too much.

Hey-up Slang expression to attract attention.

his stand on the chair i.e. in the cage which carries the miners to the top of the shaft.

a grey, dismal host Ironic, with some suggestion of a Biblical or military echo.

feeling sufficiently to resist temptation A subtle, economical, analysis of mood.

Her love came up hot A phrase typical of Lawrence's direct, uncompromising language.

sluthered Note the onomatopoeic content of this word.

'Han yer got a drink Morel is singularly unable to communicate his emotions, and takes refuge in voicing commonplace needs. This inarticulateness in fact directs our sympathy towards him at times.

Which made her laugh Not a correct construction, as the relative cannot begin a sentence. Much of *Sons and Lovers* gives the impression of being written without much attention to correctness or to conventional style. This is not surprising, since Lawrence regarded himself as a rebel; he was bent on conveying emotions and reactions, and he regarded formal diction as a barrier rather than anything else. Here he stands in contradistinction to Henry James.

he wanted to kiss her . . . she half wanted him to kiss her This shows how small is the line that divides them really.

manse Ecclesiastical residence.

the wedding at Cana The marriage attended by Jesus (John, 2,1–2).

When He changed The whole paragraph is charged with Lawrence's irony, and provides an effective contrast once Morel enters. The clergyman represents the ideal, Morel the reality, of love.

barkled up Caked, encrusted, and hence, dried.

dingin' away Onomatopoeic again.

And then she sat down and laughed The sudden onset of a form of hysteria.

like the bed of a sea of light A mixed but effective metaphor, vivid and simple.

the softly-woven sky A metaphorical description showing acute poetic sensibility.

like black flakes on a slow vortex Again very effective, because of the colour and idea of being drawn into a whirlpool which birds circling sometimes convey.

boss Protuberance.

gentlemen Even this is ironic. Mrs Morel in her loneliness, although a 'lady', is not leisured like the gentlemen who play cricket.

The sun was going down . . . went cold A superb, poetic paragraph, rich in word-painting and atmosphere, the beauty contrasting with the suffering of the woman who views the scene.

Joseph The last of Jacob's family, he had a 'coat of many colours' (Genesis, 30,24).

And at that moment . . . that she and her husband were guilty Presumably because the child, which appears sad and brooding, was not conceived in love.

I will call him 'Paul' . . . she knew not why But see note on 'the Apostle Paul', p.24, for possible subconscious reasons.

like a flash of hot fire A commonplace but effective image.

I'd wait on the dog at the door first i.e. I would far sooner serve a dog than you.

By a cruel effort of will i.e. she had to be cruel to herself, she had to suffer in order to move.

with numb paws An unobtrusive hint that Morel has behaved like an animal.

Fascinated he watched . . . and pull down the gossamer A vivid word-picture.

his manhood broke i.e. he burst into tears.

What of this child? The events have made her recur to her thoughts earlier in the evening – what is to become of a child conceived in misery rather than in love?

like a sulking dog Again the suggestion of Morel's animal nature.

ate into his spirit like rust A very effective image to stress the gradual moral corruption of Morel.

The children breathed the air that was poisoned One of many commonplace images which underline the domestic disharmony and its effects.

He always ran away from the battle with himself i.e. his moral nature, his sense of responsibility, always succumbed to his sensual nature, his wish to avoid responsibility.

gabeys Simpletons.

so fat and yet so ignominious ... like dejected ears from the knots Very effective personification, because the bundle is made to reflect the character of its owner.

Revision questions on Chapters 1–2

1 Give an account of the scene in which Morel turns his wife out into the garden.

2 Explain Mrs Morel's reactions when she is actually in the garden. What do you find unusual in the author's description?

3 Give an account of the day of Paul's birth from the standpoint of (a) Mr Morel and (b) Mrs Morel.

4 Describe the scene in which Morel interrupts the conversation between his wife and the congregational clergyman, Mr Heaton.

5 What is Mrs Morel's reaction to the birth of Paul?

6 For whom do you feel the most pity, Morel or Mrs Morel, after the scene when Mrs Morel's eye is cut by the drawer? Give reasons for your answer.

7 Do you find anything humorous in Chapter 2?

8 Explain, as fully as possible, Mrs Morel's attitude towards (a) her husband and (b) her family.

9 What do you think Walter Morel enjoys most in life? (You may, of course, refer to the day of the 'wakes', but need not confine yourself to this.)

10 Indicate the main differences in the characters of Mr and Mrs Morel.

Chapter 3 The Casting off of Morel – the Taking on of William

Morel is sickening for an attack of inflammation of the brain, and Mrs Morel, of course, has to nurse him and look after the children as well. However, the neighbours are good to her, and she has enough money coming in from clubs, and what Morel's friends put aside for her, to keep going. For a time during his recuperation, husband and wife come closer together again. Then another child is born, a boy; he is named Arthur, and he loves his father from the beginning.

Meanwhile the others are growing up, and there is another unpleasant incident when William, who is alleged to have mistreated another boy, is almost assaulted by Morel. Mrs Morel's strength of character triumphs, and she dares him to strike William; from then on Morel is, secretly, afraid of her.

When the children are old enough to be left, Mrs Morel joins the Women's Guild; this is a real outlet for her intellectual nature, for she reads papers to the other members from time to time. She battles to stop William going down the pit, wins, and gets him an office job. William has always been good at everything. He is promoted and begins to mix with the bourgeois of Bestwood. William is popular, good-looking and generous, and attractive to girls, many of whom come to call for him at his home. He also inherits from his father, somewhat to his mother's disgust, a love of dancing. Later William gets a better post in Nottingham, and then a much better one in London. He leaves home to start his new life.

winder Something that takes one's breath away, a marvellous story.

mardy Self-pitying, miserable, moaning. Common dialect slang in the Midlands and North.

but it was like a tide that scarcely rose An unobtrusive image which is connected with the ebb of Mrs Morel's feelings for her husband.

There was the halt . . . more or less a husk A fine paragraph in which the way of nature and time is compared to the way of human life.

like a man pitching quoits It is almost as if this is an image left over from the ebb and tide images used earlier.

She saw him a man . . . glow again for her The coming intensity of Mrs Morel's possessiveness is hinted at here.

barm-man Man selling yeast. In those days, housewives baked their own bread.

cobbler Horse-chestnut, 'conker'.

'Adam and Eve an' pinch-me . . . got saved' A proverbial joke, still practised.

snipey vixen A term of disrespect implying malicious interference.

milord A convenient form of irony for the husband – the lord and master.

stool-harsed A colloquial term meaning 'sitting on his bottom'.

truck-end Bottom.

bourgeois Originally the shop-keeping middle-class. Here it means the middle-class generally.

flower-like ladies, most of whom lived like cut blooms The image is particularly apt, since William is to attach himself to a 'cut bloom' in his romantic way – and to pay for it with his life, for his death results, in part at least, for his worry over her.

errant swain Lawrence often chooses words deliberately because of their ironic overtones. Here the language, with its medieval flavour, indicates the divorce from reality which is to characterize William's adventures in love.

brazen baggages Bold, good-for-nothing girls. The language indicates Mrs Morel's capacity for jealousy, later to be fully shown towards Miriam.

mater This word, instead of 'Mother' or 'Mum', reflects what the boys think of their mother (she is a 'lady'); perhaps it also stresses their superiority to their own class.

Almost she lived by him ... nearly all himself away Notice how the short sentences of this paragraph, each stressing an aspect of Mrs Morel's reactions, reflect the state of worry she is in.

Postle Presumably an abbreviation of 'Apostle', and hence a natural nickname for Paul. Beatrice Wyld also refers to him by this name. (See 8, 250,251.)

He was scarcely conscious that she was so miserable An ironic reminder of how little we know of the inner feelings even of those close to us.

Croesus A King of Lydia of the 6th century BC, celebrated for his abundant wealth.

Lafayette The Marquis of Lafayette took part in the American War of Independence and in the French Revolution; he wished to establish a Republic, with the minimum of violence, on American lines.

transpires Really means 'to send off in vapour', but has come to be used, incorrectly, as a synonym for 'happen'.

Chapter 4 The Young Life of Paul

Paul's early life is described – his closeness to Annie, and one or two incidents from their childhood. In particular Lawrence describes the symbolic sacrifice of Annie's doll Arabella, which parallels the sacrifice of Mrs Morel to Morel. The family are united against the father, and on one specific occasion Mrs Morel has to prevent an open fight between William and Morel.

When William is older, the family take another house on the brow of the hill. In front of the house there is an old ash-tree, easily swayed by the wind, and Paul often hears its 'shrieks and cries' as he lies sleepless waiting for his father to return home drunk. The anxiety of the children whenever their father stops out to drink – and this is often – is well conveyed.

Paul wins a prize in a child's paper competition, and Mrs Morel makes him tell his father. There follows an account of the happy times with the father in his home – times when he gets the children to help him with odd jobs, because he is a good domestic handyman. In this way Lawrence conveys sympathy for Morel, so that the picture we are shown is not a one-sided one. In fact Morel has some endearing qualities, not the least of which is his ability to tell stories of the pit where he works. Paul's delicacy as a child often recurs in the narrative, and this delicacy naturally brings him closer to his mother. Yet the tenderness of Morel when his son is sick is also stressed, a tenderness which, however, is not appreciated by Paul.

The Morels are often poor, and the children take great delight in helping economically, and frequently go out early to pick mushrooms. Among other things, Paul also has to fetch his father's money on Fridays, and it is on these occasions that his acute sensitivity is revealed. The description of a typical paying-out is laced with the author's observation and humour, yet we feel the abject condition of the men as well. Paul tells his mother that he won't be going any more but she soothes him out of his mood. On Friday nights Mrs Morel goes to market, whenever she can buying small things – the example given is a little dish – for the family. Paul helps her with cakes and bread, and takes a great interest in things domestic.

The winter evenings when the young Morels go out to play with other children are also described, so that the overall effect is of much happiness as well as the misery endured on account of the drunkenness of Morel. One particular autumn when there is short time in the pits and William has gone to work in London they are very poor, but they look forward to Christmas when William is to return. The children waiting for his train, the parents on edge, the triumph of his arrival and his generosity to his family, all these are conveyed with a superb sense of the atmosphere of excitement and happiness.

'flybie-skybie' A giddy, thoughtless, flighty person (generally applied to a woman).

lerky A noisy children's game in which a tin is kicked out of a ring.

antimacassar A covering usually placed over the backs or arms of chairs to protect them from grease.

'Let's make a sacrifice of Arabella' This seems to be symbolic, as explained above. However, Lawrence implied further on that Paul has to get rid of the doll because he has broken it, and the sacrifice will therefore rid him of his guilt.

chelp Chatter.

jockey Lad.

which spread out . . . or a clamp-shell Notice the imaginative force of the image. A clamp-shell is simply a bivalve shell-fish.

a huge old ash-tree This plays a symbolic part in the novel. It is variously regarded by Paul and his father, and is mentioned at moments of domestic crisis in the house. The ash-tree is personified to add force to its presence. On the nights when Morel comes home drunk the children listen to its shrieks and cries, and Lawrence suggests that the tree and its reactions parallel the sufferings of Mrs Morel at the hands of her husband.

one tight place of anxiety . . . which showed all their lives i.e., they never lost the childhood worry over their mother and father.

the children suffered with her This shows how close-knit the family was.

the great trough of twilight An observant, sweeping image.

The collier's small, mean head Notice that the description, with its bias, comes from the bitter consciousness of Paul.

the scotch in the smooth, happy machinery of the home Again notice that the image is an industrial one. A scotch is a wedge or block placed before the wheel.

He had denied the God in him This appears to mean that he has betrayed himself, he has abused the sacred trust of parenthood.

iron goose Smoothing-iron with handle shaped like the neck of a goose.

like a stalk of gold A vivid nature image.

Taffy Proverbial nickname for a Welshman.

fawce False, cunning.

slives Moves quickly or slyly.

that cadin' That spoilt one (usually applied to a child).

snap-time Time for him to eat his brandy-snap.

snied Over-run.

a little ball of spit bounded, raced off the dark glossy surfae Notice the vividness and economy of the word-picture.

kicking against the pricks A proverbial saying meaning 'to resist to one's own disadvantage'. (Originally from Acts, 9,5 and 16,140.)

He was always very gentle Another point in Morel's favour.

knits the sleep An unconscious echo of Macbeth's 'sleep that knits up the ravell'd sleave of care' (*Macbeth*, II,2,36).

The snowflakes suddenly arriving on the window-pane . . . over the great whiteness A beautiful paragraph, full of vivid word-pictures which in some strange way seem to come from the heightened imagination of the convalescent Paul.

the joy of accepting something straight from the hand of Nature The simple personification and the sentiment expressed combine to convey Lawrence's deep love for natural things.

frumenty Hulled wheat boiled in milk and seasoned with cinnamon or sugar.

in a curious tone, as of a woman accepting a love-token Certainly she is accepting a love-token, and we are drawn immediately to ponder the deliberate ambiguity of the title of the novel.

patriarch, patriarchal Lawrence's irony here, since Mr Braithwaite is not a venerable old man or the father of a tribe, except in a commercial sense.

if he puts his foot through yer i.e. kicks you very hard (for saying what you were advised to say). Rather sharp humour.

An' cheek an' impidence Again, sharp, working-class humour.

bested me Got here before me.

de haut en bas (fr.) The landlady looks him up and down.

clear, fierce morality In this case, his determination not to drink.

drops his 'h's' . . . says 'You was' Indications, perhaps, of Paul's inherent snobbery.

made her sleeping soul lift up its head Personification as a means of giving independent life is a commonplace with Lawrence.

gallivanted i.e. gadded about, went out and enjoyed herself.

gabey See note p.29.

nubbly Lumpy, knobbly.

come down . . . pick-me-up Paul is playing on words. He means that it looks rather battered and needs rejuvenating.

jowl Strike a blow.

scrattlin' Scraping.

the big red moon . . . like a great bird Note the vividness of the image and also how completely Lawrence has got inside the mind of Paul.

the Bible, that the moon should be turned to blood See 1 Chronicles, xxiii,31.

'My shoes are made of Spanish leather . . . I wash myself in milk' A proverbial song.

the great scallop of the world An image used earlier (see p.24), though somewhat differently.

like the black crest of a newt The large compared to the small without any loss of effect.

like fine black crape Acute observation again.

flig Flying, leaping.

holled i.e. shouted (at me).

he was like her knight who wore her favour in the battle This is part of an imagery sequence in *Sons and Lovers* which carries a particular irony. It is also pathetic.

He sat, quite awkward with excitement Again the author is allowing a swing of the reader's sympathy towards Morel.

ill-sitting hen Uncomfortable, not hatching its eggs properly, not still.

The ash-tree moaned outside See note on 'a huge old ash-tree', p.33.

Gladstone bag A kind of light portmanteau, named after W. E. Gladstone, the eminent Victorian Prime Minister.

Revision questions on Chapters 3–4

1 Describe how the family exist when Morel is not working.

2 How does Mrs Morel 'relax'? Is this in any way connected with her ambitions for William?

3 Trace William's career from his schooldays to his finally getting the job in London. Does Mrs Morel demonstrate any possessive love for him during this time?

4 What is the significance of (*a*) Annie's doll Arabella and (*b*) the ash-tree in the life of Paul?

5 Give an account of the children's reactions to the disagreements between their father and mother.

6 Is Morel a good father in any ways? Give reasons for your answer.

7 Give three examples of Paul's sensitivity from Chapter 4.

8 Write an account of the family's reactions before and after the return of William for Christmas.

9 Although husband and wife are not close, show how Mrs Morel is a good wife to her husband.

10 How does Mrs Morel demonstrate that she has much more character than her husband?

Chapter 5 Paul Launches into Life

About a year after William goes to London, Morel has an accident at the pit. He breaks his leg, and Mrs Morel visits him in hospital. The children realize only too keenly her anxiety and worry with the breadwinner incapacitated, though as it happens they are not badly off for money while Morel is in hospital. In a critical condition for a time, Morel recovers, though he is a poor patient.

Paul is now fourteen years old, very sensitive indeed, and has to begin looking for work. William writes his first letter of application for him and, meanwhile, writes home to tell his mother all about his London life and, more particularly, his London love. Paul applies to Thomas Jordan, Manufacturer of Surgical Appliances, in Nottingham, for a post. He goes with his mother to Nottingham for the interview with Mr Jordan. For Mrs Morel and her son this is an intimate day out, and something of an adventure as well. Both of them are very excited.

The interview is not without humour, and Paul gets the position despite his inability to translate an order from the French. Afterwards he and his mother have lunch together, and arrangements are made for Paul to travel in every day to Jordan's. William, meanwhile, has committed himself to a girl in London who is taking every penny of his money, so that he has ceased to send any home for some time.

It is a struggle to get Paul to Jordan's to begin with because of his small wage, but he quickly settles down despite his sensitivity. He gets on well with his immediate superior, Mr Pappleworth, and also with the girls, particularly the hunchback, Fanny. The various girls with whom Paul works are described, and – occasionally – an incident from the daily routine which he follows. Although the hours are very long, Paul gains a sense of security in his work, so that he feels that even the 'ash-tree seemed a friend now'. Every night he relates the day's experiences to his mother.

getting easy a bit at last Just as things were beginning to improve.

granite setts Granite blocks to pave a road, e.g. on a hill, where wear and tear was hard. Cf. the 'granite cobbles', 10,316.

And she . . . supporting her From now on the deepening bond of sympathy between mother and son is stressed, and after the death of William it becomes the most important thing in both of their lives.

mortification Spread of gangrene in the injured limb.

her little rocking chair . . . when the first baby was coming Notice that at this moment of crisis Lawrence reminds the reader of a time when the Morels were happy and much closer together than they are now.

They were an old pair of Paul's A quiet underlining of the economy Mrs Morel has to employ.

when there was any clog . . . stupid and ugly An easy and natural use of a machinery image to describe a human reaction, one of Lawrence's favourite devices. The continuation of this extract reveals the author's insight into human motives, a consummate ability to look beneath the superficial reflex.

this world's gear Equipment, colloquially, 'as far as this world is concerned'.

his whole being was knotted This commonplace image is frequently used to stress Paul's inner torments.

Already he was a prisoner of industrialism A deeply felt author-pronouncement. Lawrence sees Paul dependent on the needs of society, not free to develop his own interests.

His freedom in the beloved home valley was going now A considered stress of the importance of 'roots' to the individual, and a capturing of the moment of change which we all experience when we break away from the old – if only during working hours – and face the new.

like beans in a burst bean-pod A typically fresh and observant image.

a great gun Quite a success. William begins to feel that nothing is beyond him.

spin giddily on the quick current of the new life An image from natural observation, but ironically used when we consider how quickly William becomes dizzy, with tragic results for himself.

Tall and elegant . . . till you see her The triteness of the description – stale images, the sentimental tone, serve to underline the misguided nature of William's feelings.

with something screwed up tight inside him An image connected with the 'knot' sequence used to indicate Paul's sensitivity.

She was gay . . . love of her The irony is that neither realizes the obsessive quality of the love that rules their lives. Mrs Morel has never had a 'lover' in the true sense of the term, and Paul can never give himself to a woman because of the love he bears his mother.

a rare, intimate smile, beautiful with brightness and love See note above, which explains Mrs Morel's feelings.

feeling the excitement of lovers having an adventure together In a sense, of course, they are.

It's just like Venice Pathetic in view of the fact that both Paul and his mother are 'prisoners of industrialism'.

into the jaws of the dragon An image expressive of their apprehension, but it is not in the knight/damsel sequence.

Charles I mounted his scaffold with a lighter heart Charles I was executed on 30 January 1649, and his bravery and dignity at the time have been justly celebrated, notably by the poet Marvell. This reference is strangely out of place, and is presumably meant to be humorous. It is certainly not witty and adds nothing to our understanding of Paul.

of a pomeranian dog . . . with one ear up, as it were Lawrence likes to work up a small sequence of two or more images. Pomeranian dogs are very small, with long silky hair and pointed muzzles.

with that peculiar shut-off look ... favour of others Acute observation on the part of Lawrence.

horse-trams i.e. old-fashioned tram-cars, which were pulled by horses.

the Castle on its buff ... of delicate sunshine Lawrence is very adept at catching a moment and perpetuating it in a memorable word-picture.

Louisa Lily Denys Western This reeling-off of all the Christian names is an ironic aside at the girl's pretentiousness.

chiffonier A movable low cupboard with a sideboard top.

'An' come again to-morrer' There is no accurate rendering of Morel's reaction. He is being satirical because of the number of names.

He loved it with its bars of yellow across Paul is essentially sentimental about associations and things.

From the ash-tree ... home had never pulled at him so powerfully A vivid blending of beautiful natural description and mood.

they were derived from her ... their works also would be hers This is the major part of her fulfilment; it is the substitute for love of her husband.

smoking-cap i.e. of an ornamental kind, normally worn while one smoked.

chlorodyne A patent medicine, narcotic plus anodyne.

doggy It is not quite clear whether this is intended to mean 'devoted to dogs' (later Pappleworth produces a Yorkshire terrier), or whether it is a slang expression, perhaps equivalent to 'a gay dog' (somewhat disreputably applied).

'cute i.e. acute.

strike my bob A exclamation rather meaningless – a bob is a blow.

I'd a' eaten 'em I would certainly have finished them by now.

Only wait for you A satirical, humorous, perhaps flirtatious remark.

prime State of highest perfection (here said satirically).

'Two Little Girls in Blue' A popular song of the period.

don't make a softy of him Slang for 'Do not make him effeminate'.

Au revoy Mispronunciation of '*au revoir*' (Fr.) meaning 'Goodbye' – till we meet again.

'saloon bar' i.e. friendly and talkative, almost as if drink had loosened his tongue.

Elaine in the 'Idylls of the King' Paul is referring to Tennyson's collection of poems based on Arthurian legends.

there was a patch of lights at Bulwell ... like hot breath on the clouds ... shone like swarms of glittering living things ... violated by a great train A succession of brilliant word-pictures, revealing Lawrence's poetic tendencies.

The ash-tree seemed a friend now It is symbolic of home and the new-found security of his position at Jordan's.

His life story ... her own life i.e. it is romantic, but it further stresses the bond between mother and son.

Chapter 6 Death in the Family

This chapter opens with a description of the growing up of Arthur, the friction between the latter and his father, and the clinging of Mrs Morel to Paul once Arthur goes to live in Nottingham to attend the High School. Meanwhile William becomes engaged to Gyp, and continues to squander most of his money on her. He brings her home for Christmas, and a vivid contrast is provided with that first Christmas when he came home loaded with the family presents. The girl is irresponsible and condescends to the Morels, and it is obvious that William realizes her shortcomings but has not the strength of will to break away from her. He pities her and has long conversations with Mrs Morel, who notices a decline in his health; in personality he is no longer the lively character he once was.

Paul's wages are increased, and on one of his half-days he and his mother go off to see the Leivers, who have moved to a new farm. It is an event in both their lives. They have a wonderful walk there and Paul picks flowers for his mother. They also meet the sad Mrs Leivers and her daughter Miriam, aged 14. The boys and Mr Leivers join them for tea, and afterwards the youngsters play games. Miriam here reveals her extreme sensitivity and self-consciousness. Paul becomes friendly with her.

At Whitsun, William and his fiancée come home again. Things have not improved – William is more gaunt than ever – and once again the girl treats Annie like a slave, and shows the superficial, vain side of her nature. The lovers often disagree, and Mrs Morel can see quite clearly that they should not marry. William. however, though full of criticism of his beloved, cannot bring himself to break with her. At the same time, some of the things he says to the girl succeed in enraging his mother. As the year wears on William has a premonition that he will die.

Shortly after his return to London he is stricken with pneumonia; his mother hurries to him, but he dies. Morel goes to London, and the body of William is brought home. Paul, sad himself, is appalled at the effect of the death on his mother, who is interested only in the memory of the dead. Then Paul gets pneumonia; Mrs Morel is brought to the realization of his need for her, and nurses him through the crisis. At Christmas a chatty note arrives from the dead William's fiancée.

the flower of the family An image used of his father in his young manhood (Chapter 1).

And his father . . . he came to detest Lawrence is here expressing one of the commonplaces of human nature – our later rejection of what we once loved.

slow ruin A vivid phrase to describe physical decline.

gen Given.

kissing-bunch A bunch of holly, mistletoe, evergreens etc., hung up at Christmas.

Tha's let on me! You've got here before me.

chattered from fear Although Gyp is an unsympathetic character, Lawrence shows by touches like this that he has not altogether withdrawn his sympathy from her.

Miss Western was the princess It is a little ironic that Miriam would wish to be thought of in this way.

winder! see note p.30.

felt he was the father of princes and princesses The irony is that this is a fairy-tale with a most unhappy ending.

The old brick wall . . . green shoulders proudly Note the vivid colour effects, and the unobtrusive personification.

bobby-dazzler Brilliant effect (Slang).

"Doesn't *that* little person fancy herself!" Paul's way of really flattering his mother and showing a pride in her.

looking as if she was wrapped in burnt paper An effective, commonplace image.

'I'm afraid you'll have to put up with one' A poignant reminder that they will grow even farther apart later on.

'And so's the pit . . . with men's hands, all of them' This whole sequence, as Paul sketches, shows his sensitive imagination.

the bluebells stood in pools of azure A beautiful effect of limpid colour.

his heart hurt with love Paul often gets this sensation, particularly when he is alone with his mother at some moment of intimate connection between them.

guelder-roses Shrubs with round bundles of white flowers, snowball-trees.

with a golden-brown moustache . . . against the weather Again the emphasis is on colour, a sudden word-picture.

mardy-kid Frightened (miserable) child. The implication is that Miriam is uncooperative.

tweedle Whistle or pipe, with different modulations of tone.

Not such a clown . . . silently A proverbial rhyme.

'Lady of the Lake' It is not clear whether Miriam means Ellen Douglas, the heroine of Scott's *Lady of the Lake*, a long poem, or Vivien, the enchantress of Tennyson's *Idylls of the King*.

penny daisies . . . like laughter An exquisite image indicating nature's abundance and the happiness one experiences in it. (Ragged robin are small, pink, wayside flowers.)

baffled look of misery and fierce appreciation The well-known analogy of love and hate is perhaps appropriate here.

the billing and twittering lover A phrase scathing in its irony.

wessel-brained Weak-brained.

marrons glacés Chestnuts iced with sugar.

lookout i.e. outlook.

her soul felt lamed in itself An unobtrusive, expressive image.

At two o'clock . . . he died Note the terrible economy of the description which heightens the shock.

heatstocks Frames over shafts, carrying the pulleys for hoisting cables.

carfle A load of coal which has been cut away.

And William is dead Note how completely Lawrence has captured the incoherence of the young man's reactions.

peaked Sharp-featured, pinched.

They were walking in silence . . . apart Even at this moment of terrible suffering, they cannot be brought together.

that rode like sorrow on their living flesh A very effective contrast.

my son – my son! Symbolic of Mrs Morel's grief at her loss, but the words are repeated exactly when she feels that she is going to lose Paul.

Like a monument . . . His mother was stroking the polished wood Both emphasize that death is absolute, and that William is gone forever.

'I should have watched the living, not the dead' Mrs Morel does not repeat the mistake.

Revision questions on Chapters 5–6

1 Describe the family's reaction to their father's accident.

2 Give an account of the chief events in the day out that Mrs Morel and Paul have in Nottingham when Paul is interviewed at Jordan's.

3 What do you find humorous in Paul's interview with Mr Jordan?

4 Describe Paul's early experiences at Jordan's.

5 What signs are there that Paul is drawing ever closer to his mother?

6 Describe 'Gyp's' first visit to the Morel household.

7 Would you describe William as a strong or weak character? Give reasons for your answer.

8 Give a brief account of the family at Willey Farm.

9 What signs are there that William is declining rapidly in health?

10 Give an account of Paul's reactions to his brother's death.

Part 2

Chapter 7 Lad-and-Girl Love

A description of Paul's visits to Willey Farm, his friendship with the Leivers family, and of Miriam's mystical relationship with her mother. All the details on Miriam are filled in – her religious fervour, her hatred of her menial position in relation to her brothers, her beauty and her developing feelings for Paul. Miriam lives largely in a dream-world and fails to attend to everyday practical things such as the boiling of potatoes. She is humiliated by the boys' ridicule of her impractical nature. Paul senses the intense feelings in the house which make the boys sneer at something that is not really important. Paul is greatly influenced by Mrs Leivers who, with Miriam, does much to help and sustain him after his illness and the long process of convalescence. He also becomes friendly with the brothers, whose rudeness is only superficial. Miriam, however, makes a point of seeking him out. He tells her that she is always sad, and he notices that her love for her young brother is exclusively possessive; he feels that he hates her for this.

Miriam is physically afraid, and very dissatisfied with her lot in life. Paul agrees to teach her mathematics and French, but although he does so he finds her lacking in self-confidence, self-absorbed, and owing to this, slow. She has too much 'soul' for him, and on these occasions he goes off with her brother Edgar, who is rational where Miriam is emotional. Paul continues with his painting and sketching, showing his efforts to Miriam. The amount of time he spends with her occasions words between Paul and his mother. Mrs Morel recognizes the nature of Miriam's love – that she wants to possess Paul, or at least his soul. Neither of them will acknowledge that love is growing between them though.

Once when Paul organizes a walk for a group of young people he finds that Miriam does not fit in with them. Miriam has a sense of personal religion which is so strongly developed that she is incapable of living without it – she even asks God to let her stop loving Paul if it is not right that she should. She cannot have a normal relationship with Paul – she is incapable of ordinary physical love. Miriam stops calling for Paul on Thursday evenings because she feels that she has been slighted by his family. However, she later goes on holiday with the family, and Mrs Morel comes to dislike her because she feels that Miriam is making Paul priggish and irritable. Paul is (unknowingly) more and more frustrated at his inability to enjoy a physical relationship with Miriam.

A Walter Scott heroine . . . in their caps Scott's novels cover a variety of historical periods, they are essentially romantic in tone and colouring, and they are unreal in the sense that they do not reflect everyday, common life. There is distinct irony in this, since Miriam rarely exists on a real plane herself.

princess turned into a swine-girl A commonplace situation in fairy tales and the like. The princess usually marries the prince, who may well be a swineherd in disguise! Once again the irony is apparent.

They were both . . . burned out the western sky This passage is the key to Miriam's character.

Ediths . . . Guy Mannerings All heroines and heroes of Scott's novels.

'Colomba' A famous novel by Prosper Merimée (1840).

'Voyage autour de ma Chambre' By Xavier de Maistre (1763–1852), a now largely forgotten classic.

shy, wild, quiveringly sensitive thing The description is almost that of an animal, and Miriam's reactions – though she hates real-life experiences like birth – do much to bear it out.

her eyes dilating suddenly like an ecstasy An ominous indication of Miriam's capacity for religious rapture.

strange, almost rhapsodic way in which the girl moved about Again showing that Miriam lives in a private world of mystical – and emotional – experience. This is emphasized in the rest of this paragraph.

King Cophetua's beggar-maid King Cophetua, an imaginary King in Africa, who married a beggar-girl and lived happily ever after with her.

The girl stiffened as if from a blow The image conveys the suddenness with which Miriam is brought back to reality – and it also reveals her capacity for humiliation.

like some saint out of place at the brutal board This she intends Miriam at least to see, and it helps explain Miriam's own attitude.

The mother exalted everything . . . to the plane of a religious trust Again this has its effect upon Miriam, whose reaction is to ignore the practical because of her own obsession with the spiritual.

they scorned . . . intercourse i.e. they were unable to enter into the give-or-take of life; everything was too important, too intense.

scalloped splashes of gold A favourite Lawrence image.

Anthropomorphic Attributing human form or personality to God.

And she was . . . or else an ugly, cruel thing A definitive statement on Miriam's nature and beliefs.

Mrs Leivers . . . his disciples In view of the fact that he is 'Paul', the term 'disciples' carries its own irony.

'les derniers fils d'une race épuisée' The last sons of a vanquished race (Fr).

Men have such different standards of worth from women Lawrence rarely intervenes in the narrative, but here he ventures a pronouncement.

as if he were lying on some force An effective image which appears to come from Miriam's consciousness.

Down to her bowels . . . hot pain These are typical of Lawrence when he wishes to convey emotional sensations – he uses simple, direct, often outspoken physical terms which arrest the attention by their bluntness.

Only this shimmeriness . . . inside really Paul is trying to convey his own attempts to paint the real living content as against the outward shape of it which is relatively easy to trace.

even your joy . . . sadness An image which shows Miriam's lack of naturalness – she rarely, if ever, laughs.

one of Reynold's 'Choir of Angels' Reference to a picture by the famous portrait painter, Sir Joshua Reynolds.

dark as a dark church . . . conflagration Note how appropriate the images are to the two sides of Miriam's religiosity – her spiritual devotion and her ecstatic raptures.

She might have been . . . Jesus was dead The subject obsessed Lawrence, and he wrote what amounts to a retelling of the resurrection in *The Man Who Died*.

the half-laugh that comes of fear Acute observation.

pecked into lace by the fowls Images come readily to Lawrence, and they are always meaningful and arresting.

'You don't learn Algebra with your blessed soul' Miriam's incapacity for objective effort is revealed by this remark of Paul's.

burst like a bubble surcharged An effective image, because Miriam's intense spirituality places a burden on Paul's self-control, which occasionally gives way.

eager, silent, as it were, blind face The force of the last adjective cannot be overemphasized. Miriam is blind because she is incapable of seeing what she does not want to see.

till he had seen it . . . something holy Miriam's mystical conception here makes love as most mortals understand it impossible. Always things are seen from her side and her side only – and here she is making Paul what she wants to make him – her sharer in religious experience.

the sky in front, like mother-of-pearl A very observant word-picture.

It was very still . . . and touched them in worship The whole of this
should be read carefully. It contains some fine images and natural
description and also conveys the oppressive atmosphere which Miriam
on the edge of ecstasy always seems to generate.

There was a cool scent of ivory roses . . . anxious and imprisoned A
finely economical piece of writing. The virginity of the roses parallels
Miriam's, and Paul is uncomfortable not only because of Miriam's
rapture, but also because he has no human, physical contact with her.

gaby Simpleton.

bits of lads and girls courting Note this overt indication of Mrs Morel's
jealousy.

spoon Common slang at the turn of the century, meaning 'behave
amorously'.

'one of the deep sort' A slang expression, perhaps equivalent to the
proverbial 'Still waters run deep'. Miriam is 'deep', her motives and
emotions are not as readily seen and understood as are those of most
people.

psychical ripeness was much behind even the physical Mental and
spiritual development came even later than their physical maturity.

Paul took his pitch from her Equivalent to 'took his cue' from her,
followed her lead in deciding what should or should not be discussed.

an utterly blanched and chaste fashion The adjectives reflect
Lawrence's irony at their purity, their lack of physical passion.

kested Beaten to it.

buzz An onomatopoeic word which conveys the noise and movement
of the train.

Miriam loitered behind, alone . . . upon the leaves The whole
paragraph is saturated with Miriam's excessive spirituality and her
intense reactions to nature.

Quivering as at some 'annunciation' Lawrence's irony at Miriam's
expense frequently takes the form of religious terminology.

The words went through Miriam like a blade The suddenness and
economy of the image reflect the impressionability of Miriam.

All his latent mysticism quivered into life Paul is keenly aware of
atmosphere, spiritual or natural, and his friendship with Miriam takes
him to places where his capacity for spiritual experience is brought
out.

in the purest manner of chivalry Part of the imagery sequence which
has Paul as a knight. There is a certain irony in it, and this image
appears to come from Miriam's consciousness.

Mary Queen of Scots Executed in 1587 for taking part in a conspiracy
to usurp the throne from Elizabeth I. There is a self-indulgence in
Miriam's association here – she really likes to think of sad occasions.

**But the meadow was bathed . . . and it was seldom that he gave her any
sign ... and the place was golden as a vision** Note the Biblical echoes
which indicate so directly the nature of Miriam's response.

Veronese's 'St Catherine' Paolo Veronese (1525–88), a painter of the Venetian school.

seedy Not feeling well, not in good health.

But there was a serpent in her Eden Ever-present irony in the reference, because Miriam's temptation is purely spiritual and self-dramatic.

Then she fell into that rapture . . . was sacrificed Lawrence is here criticizing the quality of Miriam's religious experience, and disapproves, just as Paul disapproves, of the personal intensity of it.

platonic friendship Derived from Plato, the Greek philosopher, it means purely spiritual love for a member of the opposite sex.

internecine Mutually destructive, here referring to the spiritual and physical halves of Paul.

Jean Ingelow . . . Mablethorpe An English poetess (1820–97), and the poem referred to is *High Tide on the Coast of Lincolnshire*. She would make interesting reading for Miriam, for much of her poetry is religious and devotional. *The Brides of Enderby* was a folktune rung on the bells as a danger signal, probably because of its lamenting air.

'The Flowers o' the Forest' A traditional Scots poem by the eighteenth-century poetess Jean Elliot. There are other versions, and the associations of the poem are to the dead in battle who will never return.

'Coons' An entertainment, very popular at coastal resorts at the turn of the century, and still enjoying a certain popularity today. Minstrels exaggeratedly disguised as Blacks performed song and dance routines, generally based on folk songs from the deep South. The accompanists would usually play banjos.

some sad Botticelli angel Botticelli (1444–1510) was a celebrated painter of the Florentine school, and the best known examples of his art deal with religious subjects.

Gothic . . . Norman The difference in the two types of architecture is defined, albeit imaginatively and poetically, by Paul in this paragraph.

The whole of his blood seemed to burst into flame . . . the ridge of the sandhills Paul is moved to want Miriam physically, but she is unable to comprehend this, 'she shrank in her convulsed, coiled torture from the thought of such a thing', and his desires had been 'suppressed into a shame'.

Chapter 8 Strife in Love

This chapter opens with the exciting news that Arthur has enlisted in the Army, purely on the spur of the moment. Mrs Morel goes to Derby to see him, and frets greatly over him. Meanwhile, Paul wins two first-prize awards in an exhibition of students' work. His mother is overjoyed and, of course, very proud, and several times during the exhibition she goes to see the pictures unknown to Paul.

One day Paul meets Miriam in Nottingham with her friend, Clara Dawes. Some account is given of Clara and of her husband – from whom she is separated – Baxter Dawes, who works at the factory and has already crossed swords with Paul. Later Paul and Miriam discuss Clara Dawes, and though Paul criticizes her it is obvious that he finds her intriguing.

Paul continues to see Miriam regularly, but their relationship remains on the same unconsummated level. Paul at this stage begins to question the orthodox creed, and his attacks on it invariably involve some cruelty to Miriam and her cherished beliefs. At the same time Paul is angered by his mother's failure to like Miriam, and these periods of tension lead him to stay away from her periodically. Paul is promoted at Jordan's, his wages rising to thirty shillings (£1.50) a week.

In this chapter Lawrence also describes an occasion when domestic harmony can be said to reign in the Morel household. This is on an evening when Morel and his immediate co-workers at the pit meet at his house to divide up the week's money. The temporary harmony, however, soon comes to an end when Mrs Morel receives a meagre amount from her husband.

After this Paul shows Miriam a cushion-cover he has made her, but their tête-à-tête is interrupted by another young woman – a friend of the Morels – whose racy chatter humiliates Miriam and at the same time reveals her social limitations. Paul begins giving Miriam French lessons. The latter writes to him in the form of a diary love-letter. Paul reads to her, often with the intention of hurting her because of her dumb adoration.

On this particular evening, when he returns from taking Miriam home, he finds his mother unwell and Annie angry with him. After Annie has gone to bed Paul endures a jealous diatribe from his mother, who points out to him in no uncertain terms how obsessed he is with Miriam. Mother and son are reconciled passionately when Morel enters somewhat drunk. There is a dramatic, near-violent scene between father and son, which is abruptly brought to an end when Mrs Morel faints. Next day normal life is resumed or, as Lawrence puts it, 'Everybody tried to forget the scene'.

sick of wearing the seat of a stool out i.e. tired of doing a sitting-down job.

taken the King's shilling Enlisted, a reference to an obsolete method of recruiting whereby a sergeant paid a recruit a shilling (5p) for joining up.

swell Slang for a member of the upper classes, rich, fine-looking.

agate Going on, in motion (now).

Not for nothing had been her struggle The inverted word-order gives this a significant emphasis.

a skin like white honey A typically vivid comparison.

pap Mashy, soft food for babies.

good little sops i.e. weak, perhaps even weak-minded here.

like a devotee A typical image to use of Miriam.

everybody feels like a disembodied spirit then This is relating the moods and reactions of humans to the state of nature – the falling of the leaves, for instance, and the first awareness of the coming winter.

Verlaine A French poet (1844–96). His lyrics were distinguished for their form rather than their content.

his blood roused to a wave of flame A favourite Lawrence image to describe the onset of physical passion.

Orion was wheeling up over the wood, his dog twinkling after him An impressive sense of the permanent, cosmic world as against the small world of mortals like Paul and Miriam.

Recklessness is almost a man's revenge on his woman Again a rare Lawrence interruption. It means that by taking risks on his bicycle Paul is releasing his frustration over Miriam.

The stars on the lake ... upon the blackness A fine sense of observation and colour.

with an intellect like a knife ... till she almost lost consciousness Two connected images which emphasize the rational, objective side of Paul as against the emotional, palpable nature of Miriam.

she will suck him up This almost implies that Miriam has a demonlike quality.

Michael Angelo (More commonly spelt Michelangelo.) Painter, sculptor, architect and poet (1474–1564), one of the greatest artists that ever lived.

Orion was for them chief in significance Miriam and Paul have a sense of mystical communion with the great constellation when they contemplate it 'intensely'.

Balzac A great French nineteenth-century novelist (1799–1850), his major work being *La Comédie Humaine*.

nesh Susceptible to cold.

sack o' faggots Bag of sticks.

hurtle Huddle, crouch, crowd.

pulamiter Almost certainly 'a weakling'.

salamander The lizard which can supposedly live in fire. Mrs Morel is therefore being sarcastic, for her husband is complaining of the cold.

tidy Fairly (dialect).

be-out Without.

Go thy way i' th'arm-chair Take yourself off to the armchair.

Wi' a rattle in it like a kettle-drum An expressive, probably proverbial, image.

Ah, an' Doomsday Ironic meaning, 'and so will death'.

guttle Swallow greedily.

whittle Tell or talk about.

Liberty's A high-class London store.

her dark eyes one flame of love Although this image is used of Paul's feelings, Miriam's love is of a different type.

Only brains to bite with A phrase meaning 'sharpness of wit'.

to share him up like Solomon's baby See 1 Kings, 3,16–27.

she felt as if her soul's history were going to be desecrated by him i.e. she thought that Paul was going to destroy her beliefs. Note the use of 'desecrate' in view of Miriam's obsession with religion.

'"*Ce matin les oiseaux . . . Il est si clair――*"' Miriam describes in this extract how she wakes at dawn having dreamt of Paul, hears all the birds singing, and wonders if he is awake and watching the beauty of it too. Once again she is hoping for a sense of communion with Paul.

She was coloured like a pomegranate for richness On the face of it, not a flattering comparison. But consider the ripeness of a pomegranate as well and the image conveys the rounded, physically attractive Miriam who is incapable of physical love. Hence Paul's frustration here and elsewhere.

She was really getting . . . next week The image suggests that Paul's teaching sustains her.

Baudelaire's 'Le Balcon' A poem by the French nineteenth-century poet, Charles Baudelaire (1821–67). His *Les Fleurs du Mal* is his best known volume of verse.

Behold her singing in the field The opening line of Wordsworth's *Solitary Reaper*.

'Fair Ines' A poem by Thomas Hood (1799–1845).

It is a beauteous evening, calm and free The opening line of a famous sonnet by Wordsworth.

Herbert Spencer (1820–1903) A celebrated nineteenth-century evolutionary philosopher.

My boy! . . . passionate love This is perhaps the closest and most intimate moment Mrs Morel and Paul experience together.

The tears were hopping down his face An unusual but effective image in view of the suddenness of what happens. Cf. a short time later when 'the tears ran down his face quietly.

Revision questions on Chapters 7–8

1 What effect do the Leivers family have on Paul?

2 Describe the main aspects of the character of Miriam Leivers. Is she in any way like Mrs Morel? Give reasons for your answer

3 What are Paul's reactions towards Miriam?

4 What effect does Mrs Morel have on her son's relationship with Miriam?

5 Give two examples from Chapter 7 of Lawrence's ability to describe nature in rare detail

6 Describe the effect on his mother of Paul's paintings winning two first prizes.

7 Is Paul cruel to Miriam? Give reasons for your answer.

8 Describe the reactions of Paul to Clara, and of Clara to Paul, judging from their behaviour.

9 Give an account of the effect Beatrice Wyld has on (*a*) Paul and (*b*) Miriam.

10 What effect does the scene with Morel have on (*a*) Paul and (*b*) Mrs Morel?

Chapter 9 Defeat of Miriam

The growing tension between Paul and Miriam, and a description of Paul's visit to the family in spring, make this chapter a natural extension of the last. Paul is so irritated by Miriam that he continues to treat her cruelly. He plays with a large bull-terrier, Bill, and takes off some of his excess energy, but soon tires of the game. Eventually he tells Miriam that he thinks they should stop seeing one another. Miriam, of course, is bewildered. She believes that his family is responsible for the break, and in the sense that Mrs Morel is such a potent influence on Paul, she is right. But the real fault lies within herself.

Paul returns to his mother, and does not go to Willey Farm for a week. When he does go he tries to persuade Miriam that she should become interested in another man. They discuss their situation, and Miriam reluctantly agrees that they should see less of one another. Paul leaves early, to the surprise of Mrs Leivers. He cannot, however, break easily with the family, and gives his friendship to Edgar; on one Sunday evening he and Miriam achieve their earlier harmony again. Later Miriam invites Clara to the farm; she is really testing Paul out to see if he can do without her.

Clara and Paul antagonize one another, but are obviously keenly aware of each other. Later the three of them go for a walk; during their outing they meet Miss Limb. There is a strong overtone of sexuality in this scene, which appears to be symbolic of frustration, and later Clara, Miriam and Paul discuss the woman's loneliness. Clara appears to be absorbed, and Paul scatters cowslips over her hair.

One day Paul takes his mother to Lincoln, and he begins to notice that she does not look well. She is unable to climb the hill to the cathedral without resting. Paul is more than ever frustrated by the knowledge of his mother's age. Meanwhile Annie and Leonard get married, Paul vows not to marry but to stay with his mother, and Arthur begins to court Beatrice Wyld, the girl who had flirted so vivaciously with Paul in front of Miriam. Paul starts to meet Clara in spite of Miriam; he and Miriam exchange letters defining their relationship, but the first phase of this is over, and he turns to Clara.

It was spring, which she loved and dreaded Miriam always feels in extremes.

clack An expressive onomatopoeic word.

a tiny ruff, reminding her of Mary Queen of Scots See note on 'Mary Queen of Scots', p.45; Miriam enjoys being associated with martyrdom. It would be true to say that she sees Paul sometimes as her executioner.

Everything looked washed, rather hard A clear, observant image of a certain kind of day in spring.

The cheeks of the flowers were greenish with cold This kind of personification shows the author's love of nature and, perhaps more important, a wide compassion.

turned up its face of gold to her Continuing the personification.

it's a bit thick – they're pretty Paul implies that she is, as usual, being excessive in her praise.

sipping the flowers with fervid kisses The picture stresses Miriam's obsession.

run hot by thwarted passion . . . like sparks from electricity A mixed image, unlike those drawn from nature, which tend to be in sequence.

the east was tender with a magenta flush A warm expression of colour, almost like a painting.

'I'll dot thee one' I'll give you a blow.

She held the keys to his soul A commonplace phrase, though it has religious associations, as one would expect with Miriam.

'Tartarin de Tarascon' By Alphonse Daudet (1840–97), a noted French novelist.

no anchor of righteousness Again the image comes from Miriam's consciousness.

Circe Perhaps an appropriate name by association for a sow, since Circe the enchantress turned Odysseus' men to swine.

Tippoo This, too, is an appropriate choice of name, since Tippoo Sahib, who was known as the 'Tiger of Mysore', resisted the British in India during the second half of the eighteenth century.

charades A game in which a word is guessed from a written or acted clue.

He was setting Agnosticism A commonplace image meaning that Paul was well on the way to believing that nothing is known or is likely to be known about the existence of God.

Renan 'Vie de Jésus' Ernest Renan was a French Biblical scholar whose *Life of Jesus* (1863), which examines the origins of Christianity, made his European reputation.

Miriam was the threshing floor . . . his beliefs An image which at least harmonizes with farming and the Leivers.

"Mary Morrison" A well-known popular song, based on a poem by Robert Burns.

the fading bluebells that might have bloomed for Deidre or Iseult The latter is the lady-love of Sir Tristram in Tennyson's *Idylls of the King*, and the former is the heroine of *The Sons of Usuach*, one of the *Three Sorrowful Stories of Erin*, in Irish legend. This begins a medieval sequence in which there is mention of knights and pavilions, and the whole is tinged with irony. Paul is mocking, and we feel that the object of the author's laughter is Miriam.

I would have 'W.S.P.U.' . . . beneath a woman rampant Here the tone of irony is most marked, and Clara is made to feel Paul's wit. W.S.P.U. stands for 'Woman's Social and Political Union', which Clara, as a suffragette, would belong to. Normally on a shield one would find a lion rampant, a term expressive of violence.

'Be good, sweet maid, and just let *me* be clever' A parody of a poem by Charles Kingsley, author of *Westward Ho!* and *The Water Babies*.

Are you home again my boy . . . She held his head in her arms against her breast This whole paragraph should be studied, because it represents a form of writing which Lawrence often employs. The woman's love for the horse is an unleashing of her repression – as Clara puts it, 'she wants a man'. But the sequence looks at Miriam and Clara as well. Miriam wants a man, but cannot give as this woman, Miss Limb, gives to the horse; Clara, unbeknown to herself at this stage, also wants a man, despite her absorption with women's rights.

It was like a roadstead covered with tall, fairy shipping A vivid word-picture.

A dead flower isn't a corpse of a flower Paul sees the beauty of the flower as being permanent.

'sturdy and lusty like little trees and like boys with fat legs' Paul is capable of vivid and meaningful language.

'Ashes to ashes, . . . the devil must' A proverbial parody of part of the burial service.

couchant (Lying) with head raised.

something in the eternal repose . . . something of the fatality The emphasis here is on time, the fact that the cathedral is old and his mother is old, and that fate cannot alter this state.

'You forget I'm a fellow taking his girl for an outing' This is one of the many constant reminders of the irony of the title of the novel.

ikey Slang for 'superior'.

Be a fantail pigeon i.e. show off.

his heart was crushed in a hot grip Passion, whether it be sexual or otherwise, is often expressed by Lawrence in images like this.

'A son's my son . . . whole of her life' A proverbial bit of doggerel.

Once he had really run the rig Once he had had his fun.

boon-companion Congenial, jolly friend.

furlough Leave.

knivey Mean, miserly.

'Shonna!' I shall not.

stood out like a brush A commonplace but effective image.

a film over her fire Beatrice is throughout – in our two meetings with her – portrayed as a passionate girl who is out to get her man.

Nay, the sky . . . the soul of Paul Morel Miriam must have a mission, and Paul is it at this stage in her life.

She could run like an Amazon We are never allowed to forget the physical appeal of Clara. The comparison is apt too, for the Amazons, famous mythical female warriors, did not accept men into their community.

you are a nun Miriam is insulted because she feels that she is part of life – she takes all life intensely, more particularly Paul – whereas a nun is shut off from life.

'Omar Khayyam' A Persian astronomer-poet who lived in the 11th– 12th centuries and whose best-known work – the Rubaiyat – was translated into English verse by Edward Fitzgerald. It has become a classic. The theme of the poem is that one should make merry and enjoy life while it lasts.

Chapter 10 Clara

The chapter opens with the exciting news that one of Paul's landscapes has won first prize in a winter exhibition at Nottingham Castle. A Major Moreton buys the picture for twenty guineas (£21), and Paul, wearing the dead William's dress-suit, begins to go out in the evenings. He grows away from Miriam, and comes to know Clara much better. One evening he calls on Clara, and meets her mother, who is a sharp and wise old woman in a rough, blunt way. He discovers that Clara does a lot of 'sweated' work at home. Paul suggests that she should come back to Jordan's, where she had once worked. He realizes, from Clara's reactions, that she is ashamed of her background, and he also learns that his own assessment of her as being 'high and mighty' was erroneous.

Susan, the overseer of the girls, has to leave Jordan's to get married, and this creates an opening for Clara. She returns to Jordan's, but she is not popular. Some remember her previous rule, and in any case she tends to be aloof and apart from the girls. Clara keeps up a veneer of coldness towards Paul, and they have one or two little exchanges and differences. Paul gets on very well with the girls in her department, and on his birthday – his twenty-third – Fanny, the long-legged hunchback, gives him a present from them of some oil-paints. Paul is overwhelmed.

Later on the same day he takes Clara out, and she reveals how much she dislikes the town. She also confides to him that the other girls do not like her and have secrets from her. Paul then tells her about the birthday present, for the girls have kept this from Clara. It is obvious that she and Paul are drawn strongly to one another physically. Clara gives Paul a volume of poetry; from then on they become more friendly, and Clara tells him the story of her marriage. Although they still have their disagreements, she and Paul go out often, and Paul tells her how things stand between himself and Miriam.

beguy! A slang expression, probably from 'By God!'.

misdoubt i.e. disbelieve.

'Yes, an' that other lad 'ud 'a done as much' The reference to William is made all the more poignant by its coming from Morel.

like a cold blade An effective image because economical and sudden, as the thrust of a sword or similar weapon is.

He had shovelled away . . . to the bedrock A connected sequence of strangely manual images with which one would not associate Paul.

the difference in people isn't in their class, but in themselves A wise, true statement.

Little Perhaps short for 'Little one', a term of endearment.

Suffragette Believer (female) in the rights of women, i.e. having the vote. Suffragettes were very active early in this century.

Unitarian A religious sect which denies the Church doctrine of the Trinity and the divinity of Christ.

she might as well be hung for a sheep as for a lamb She might as well be condemned for a big thing as for a little one while she was at it.

mausoleum An expressive usage here. The word means 'a tomb', and reflects Clara's self-consciousness about her home.

Nay, you needn't thank me Note the truth and life of the old woman's speech.

Her throat and arms were bare The sensuality of the description owes itself to Paul's immediate observation.

an anachronism i.e. not keeping time with the sharpness of her mind.

glossy and yellow as old ivory Observant with regard to colour and texture.

She'll never be satisfied till she's got wings A derogatory reference to Miriam's spirituality.

on that 'igh horse . . . one of these days A vivid image, typical of a sharp, working-class ability to extend an image in a witty and telling manner. Clara's mental and emotional suffering is accurately pinpointed in it.

Juno A Roman goddess, the wife of Jupiter, the king of heaven.

Her history . . . hidden from everyone The irony is that she is as 'deep' in a sense as Mrs Morel thinks Miriam.

gathered fruit of experience he could not attain Commonplace image.

'Lettres de Mon Moulin' By Alphonse Daudet (1840–1897).

you're terrific great shakes You think you have plenty of ability (slang).

like Penelope when she did her weaving Clara seems to inspire Paul to remember classical literature. Penelope was the wife of Ulysses, who, during her husband's absence in Troy, told her suitors that when she had finished the web she was weaving she would marry, whereupon every night she undid the web woven during the day.

spooney Soft, rather silly.

frozen meat A disparaging reference to Clara's coldness.

when my ship came in When I had a stroke of good luck.

Queen of Sheba She visited Solomon (1, Kings, 10). She was a feminine counterpart to him – a foil to his grandeur and magnificence.

feel stale india-rubber right through i.e. give and bend, unable to stand firmly.

Away beyond the boulevard . . . where the hills rose blue beyond grey A superb paragraph, which shows Lawrence's descriptive powers and his fertile imagination at work – in a scintillating range of images and word-pictures.

a vast, dark matrix of sorrow and tragedy The scene described as a womb comes from Paul's consciousness, and reflects his temporary disillusion and frustration; in fact Clara is to do much to ease this.

Somnambule? Paul is really asking if Clara performed all her actions with her husband in an unawakened state.

It fell, and the ring was quivering on the table A typical piece of symbolic writing, expressing Clara's wish to be free from the marriage tie, at least with Baxter Dawes.

Revision questions on Chapters 9–10

1 Explain why Paul feels it is necessary to break with Miriam.

2 Are your sympathies generally with Paul or with Miriam at this stage? Give reasons for your answer.

3 Explain the significance of the incident where Paul, Miriam and Clara meet Miss Limb and the horse.

4 Give an account of Paul's visit to Lincoln with his mother. What does it reveal of his character?

5 Why do you think Paul is drawn towards Clara?

6 What does Paul learn of Clara from his visit to her home? Does this knowledge reinforce his own views of her or contradict them?

7 Define Clara's attitude to the girls and Paul when she goes back to Jordan's.

8 What effect does the 'birthday incident' have on the relationship of Paul and Clara?

9 Give a short character sketch of Clara's mother, Mrs Radford.

10 Describe the atmosphere at Jordan's between Paul and the girls.

Chapter 11 The Test on Miriam

Despite the attractions of Clara, spring sees Paul's compulsive return to Miriam. His mother is amazed at his reactions, but can do nothing to stop him. Paul is determined to make love to Miriam, and circumstances provide him with the opportunity. Yet although Miriam says that she wants him to make love to her, he feels, and rightly, that she is offering herself as a sacrifice. Strangely, however, physical consummation makes him give himself up to mystical speculation, and he thinks of the afterlife. For a few days he and Miriam are able to live as man and wife, but without achieving any kind of harmony.

Eventually Paul decides to break with Miriam again. He tells his mother, who naturally welcomes it; meanwhile he has begun to go out with men friends, and also to see Clara again. One Sunday he goes to the Leivers' farm and tells Miriam that he is finishing with her. Although she follows some of his reasoning, she is bitter with him, and accuses him of always having fought her off. Paul is surprised and injured by her reaction, though intensely ashamed and shaken when he leaves her. On the way home he engages in mild flirtation with some girls in a public-house, and then goes on home to break the news to his mother. She can see just how much it has cost him.

a strong desire battling with a still stronger shyness and virginity i.e. Paul is acutely aware of his own inexperience.

and he was nearly a religion to her This is an accurate definition of Miriam's idealized fixation for Paul.

blundered . . . feminine sanctities Sexually insensitive, thinking only of their own gratification.

They preferred themselves to suffer the misery of celibacy They chose to lead a life of sexual self-denial (rather than injure the other person).

like a nun singing to heaven . . . maidenhood about her All phrases and thoughts which seem to be a prejudgement of Paul's forthcoming physical relationship with Miriam. Botticelli (1447–1510) studied under Fra Lippo Lippi, and most of his paintings are on religious subjects.

Sir Thomas More (1478–1535) Lord Chancellor of England, friend of Erasmus and author of *Utopia*, an imaginary ideal commonwealth.

she would suffer for him This in fact she does, for their physical relationship is misery for her.

The blaze struggled . . . and then was quenched A typical image to express Paul's passion.

his passion flooded him Loosely connected with the image quoted above.

not in the Gretchen way Gretchen was the guileless girl seduced by Faust in Goethe's tragedy of that name.

their chill finger-tips sending a flash down his blood Paul is extremely sensitive to atmosphere and touch, hence this reaction.

four dead birds . . . picked clear of flesh There is something powerfully symbolic about this. The birds have been shot for taking what was not theirs, and Paul is to experience a kind of death when he takes Miriam physically.

watching the gold clouds fall to pieces . . . the passion went out of the sky This beautiful passage foreshadows the rise and fall of Paul's passion for Miriam; it is a finely economical piece of symbolic writing.

I like the darkness . . . good, thick darkness But Paul is really wishing that darkness will conceal his actions.

The highest of all . . . identified with the great Being Paul reveals himself capable of mystical experience and speculation. This new trait has a distinct effect upon Miriam, as we see on the next page.

To be rid of our individuality Paul is here expressing a denial of self.

for writing introspective pieces which interested her i.e. this probably means that Miriam continued to write the personal diary kind of narrative such as she had written in French for Paul.

like a transfiguration Even in a moment of tenderness Paul, unconsciously perhaps, uses a religious image to describe Miriam.

like a creature awaiting immolation i.e. a person about to be sacrificed, an image constantly used of Miriam yielding to Paul, and 'creature' carries its own weight and diminishes Miriam's stature.

he felt that he was finally initiated He felt that he had performed the rites of his manhood (attained sexual experience).

jawing Talking.

The beauty of the night made him want to shout This whole paragraph should be read with great attention. It looks back to Mrs Morel being shut out in the garden by her drunken husband, and now her son shares a mystical experience with the lilies. Again the writing is symbolic – the overpowering atmosphere of the flowers is like the overwhelming power of Miriam over Paul. The iris represents Paul's sexual desire for her. He finds the suggestions stifling, and characteristically decides to break with Miriam. Note particularly the colour, the personification, and the compelling evocation of atmosphere.

He put the flower in his mouth . . . mouthful of petals Again this is a continuation of the symbolism. The flower is crushed, and he intends to crush Miriam.

he had landed her . . . in the lurch Paul thinks in commonplace slang terms, for he is impatient with himself.

I've had such a lark I have enjoyed myself.

Chapter 12 Passion

Paul begins to take more and more interest in his art, and believes that one day he will be a fine painter. He employs a servant-girl for his mother, and later takes his mother on holiday; immediately after finishing with Miriam, though, he turns to Clara. At first in their meetings he is half-frightened of her, but one evening plucks up courage to kiss her. He spends the weekend in a frenzy of desire, and on the Monday afternoon goes for a walk with her. Each feels the strong emotional tensions of the other. Clara questions him about his break with Miriam, and tells him that he has treated her badly.

They walk riskily along by the river, and Paul loses a parcel in it. They find a spot to themselves, having passed two fishermen. Later they get back to safety; Paul cleans Clara's boots for her, and they have tea at a little house. There is a feeling of guilt in

Clara, but Paul goes home happily to his mother. Mrs Morel is none too pleased about the fact that Paul is consorting with a married woman, for people will talk. Paul still sees Miriam, who treats him normally but questions him about Clara. Paul tries to define the lack of real love in the marriage of Clara and Baxter Dawes and, strangely, says that he believes his own mother and father shared a mutuality of passion in the first months of their marriage.

Miriam really believes that Paul will ultimately return to her, but is surprised to learn that Clara is to visit Paul's home. This visit is fraught with embarrassment for them both, but Paul is very proud of Clara. He can tell, too, that she will get on well with his mother. Morel is introduced, the atmosphere is relaxed, yet deep down Clara is fearful. Later, while they are in the garden together, Miriam arrives, and senses their harmony. She leaves bitterly, realizing that Clara is already accepted as she never was. Paul, on his return from seeing Miriam off, is angered to find his mother and Clara discussing Miriam. Later he walks with Clara, who is a little sulky that he is still friends with Miriam; this in fact provokes him into making passionate love to her. Clara says that she wants to get her train, and in fact does so, forced into running for it by a frustrated Paul.

Paul decides one evening to take Clara to the theatre. Again he is tortured by her physical beauty. He misses his train after the performance. Clara invites him to stay at her house, saying that she will sleep with her mother. The latter makes them both feel uncomfortable by her bluntness and sarcasm, but underneath she appears to have a good heart, and there is little doubt that she likes Paul. She sits up with them in order to see that Paul goes off to bed. When he does so, he lies awake waiting for the mother to come up to her bedroom. Then he goes down to Clara. Next morning at breakfast he finds that he gets on very well with Clara's mother.

my pigeon A term of endearment.
baggage Good-for-nothing.
He felt as if someone were pushing a knife in his chest Physical imagery to express emotional pain is a commonplace in Lawrence.
He was walking to the station An intent study of this paragraph will show that the short, staccato sentences reflect in their brevity the worry and anxiety and excitement which Paul is feeling – he must see Clara urgently.

And a certain heaviness . . . dips slightly in the wind Again note Lawrence's acute eye for detail in nature.

he was some attribute of her Paul is always capable of romantic, mystical excess of feeling.

The river slid by . . . like some subtle, complex creature Symbolic of the coming together of a man and a woman; there are strongly sensuous suggestions in this piece of writing.

like pillars along a great aisle An image almost evocative of a natural sanctity.

Kirke White (1785–1806). A minor poet born in Nottingham. He came under the patronage of Southey, but died of consumption after overwork.

where the flush was fusing into the honeywhite An artistic sense of colours blending, which we might expect Paul to have.

barkled Caked, encrusted.

'Why dost look so heavy?' In the tenderness of his love Paul relapses into dialect. This is natural – he has no need to be anything but himself, the language of love is the most direct and meaningful to the people concerned.

dibbling with love Like 'dabble', meaning repetition with alternating degrees of intensity.

his and Miriam's affair . . . it would die out An astute remark, but the image is ironic in view of the fact that Paul's 'fire' is unquenched by Miriam.

femme incomprise Misunderstood wife.

It almost seems to fertilize . . . and mature Paul is at a stage where he feels everything intensely. Miriam shortly after refers to it as a 'sort of baptism of fire in passion'.

twitchel Fork in the road.

a pillar . . . by night See Exodus, 13,21–2.

felt his heart contract with pain This image is always used when Paul sees his mother suffering.

seeming blown quickly by a wind at its work An image which defines Paul's mobility of mood and movement.

she felt as if a rope were taken off her ankle An image which indicates clearly how Clara has become dependent on Paul. Mrs Morel sees this and is sorry for her; her own mother rather likes Paul for the power he exerts.

'It's the end of the run with these chaps' i.e. (the bees) are coming to the end of their lives.

the bloodhound quality in Miriam Simply means that she attached herself to Paul and will not be shaken off.

stung him into a flame of hate against Miriam The usual common image, but the point is that he resents having to feel sorry for Miriam. He does not like the fact that he still feels intensely about her.

tack Topic.

speckled and spangled with lights Lawrence loves the panorama and movement of lights.

the train, like a luminous caterpillar An imaginative view of it seen at a distance.

Sarah Bernhardt A world-famous French actress (1844–1923).

'La Dame aux Camelias' A famous drama and romance by Alexandre Dumas.

the bluest of blue moons Slang for (once) in a very long time.

All the time his blood . . . white-hot waves This, and the rest of the paragraph, is redolent of Paul's physical passion for Clara.

It seemed he met a pair of brown eyes which hated him Certainly Baxter Dawes, who refers to the theatre visit in the following chapter.

fly your kites *that* high (if you are) so conceited and ambitious.

sixpenny hop A cheap dance.

crozzly Crisp.

catamaran Paul is right, but Mrs Radford is using the other meaning – a quarrelsome woman.

pierrot A reference to the kind of costume pierrots use for their performance – loose-fitting jacket, and wide-bottomed trousers.

spinning her wedding-ring Again the reflex action carries symbolic overtones – when she removes her wedding-ring, she is vulnerable to Paul.

Guyney Probably from 'Guy', a disguised form of the word 'God' used in petty oaths.

whittling . . . too-in Scraping away, adding this, taking away that (of the painting).

waxy Angry, bad-tempered.

***You* wouldn't be long in breaking your neck at a hurdle race** This is a metaphorical way of saying that Paul does things too quickly and will have to pay for the consequences.

Revision questions on Chapters 11–12

1 Why does Paul return to Miriam?

2 What is Paul's reaction after he has made love to Miriam?

3 Define Miriam's attitude when Paul does finally break with her. Do you think that she is justified in saying what she does to him?

4 What signs are there in Chapter 12 that Mrs Morel's hold on Paul is becoming stronger?

5 Examine the techniques by which Lawrence conveys the strength of Paul's physical desire for Clara.

6 How important is the background – including people – on the afternoon when Paul and Clara walk by the Trent?

7 Describe Clara's visit to the Morel household.

8 Does Clara give the impression of being frightened at the strength of her own feelings? Give reasons for your answer.

9 Give an example or two of (*a*) humour and (*b*) poetic description in Chapter 12.

10 Do you feel any pity for (*a*) Miriam or (*b*) Mrs Morel at this time?

Chapter 13 Baxter Dawes

Shortly after Paul has been to the theatre with Clara, he is talking to some friends in a public house when he is involved in an exchange with Baxter Dawes. The latter is thrown out by a professional 'chucker-out', but vows revenge against Paul. Clara is very concerned on Paul's account, but Paul is disinclined to take any precautions. The next time Paul and Baxter meet Thomas Jordan himself is caught up in their quarrel, is assaulted by Dawes (whom he has just sacked), and takes out a summons for assault. Dawes, however, is acquitted at the trial.

Meanwhile Paul and Clara continue passionately in love, though there is some degree of selfishness on Paul's side. Clara is aware of him all the time, but at Jordan's Paul concentrates on his work. He discusses Clara with his mother, but at the same time observes: 'I shall never meet the right woman while you live.' He tells Clara that he would like to go away to live with his mother, but they still experience fine moments of passion. They take a holiday together as man and wife on the Lincolnshire coast. Paul realizes that he has neither the capacity to understand Clara or himself completely, but he senses that she still feels strongly for Baxter Dawes. Clara objects that he never gives himself completely and realizes that she will never completely possess him.

Some time later Baxter passes them; Paul notices that he looks what he calls 'shady'. Lawrence describes the loss of illusion in their lovemaking, and then describes Baxter's assault on Paul one night in the dark. Paul suffers a dislocated shoulder, and then gets bronchitis. He does not really want to see Clara or Miriam, both of whom visit him. When he gets over it he starts to go out with some of his friends, and then has a holiday, calling for his mother at Annie's house in Sheffield on the way back. He finds that his mother is seriously ill with a tumour. He borrows the money for a specialist, and eventually Mrs Morel is taken home, greatly weakened. Paul is overwrought, his father is pathetic, and it is now merely a question of time before Mrs Morel dies.

Punch Bowl The name of a public-house.

lardy-da Slang for 'showing off in an affected way'.

'Tart an' all?' A slang, degrading term, asking if Paul had a girlfriend with him (at the theatre).

You shouldn't funk i.e. you should not be afraid to acknowledge.

daggeroso Given to carrying a knife.

'Put Me Among the Girls' A popular song of the period.

whipperty-snappin' i.e. like a little dog at his heels.

hung fire Held back.

'Cherchez la femme!' Look for the woman (in the case).

They had met . . . the wheel of the stars A description which reflects Paul's mystical sense of the relatedness of all that is created. This sense makes it impossible for him to accept without analysis his relationship with Clara. The reference to Adam and Eve driven out of Paradise on the same page shows how intensely Lawrence wishes the reader to see Paul and Clara in their isolation; and at the same time he is communicating his own mysticism to the reader when he says 'they knew they were only grains in the tremendous heave that lifted every grass-blade its little height, and every tree, and living thing, then why fret about themselves?'.

the baptism of fire in passion Poignantly ironic imagery, if we think of Miriam for a moment. Also see note 'his and Miriam's affair', p.60.

blind agents of a great force This certainly is connected with the idea of their being very small parts of a very large creation.

the drop of fire Clara's feelings are now being described in the same images as those used of Paul.

The morning was of a lovely limpid gold colour The whole of this paragraph is an exquisite picture, one that Paul might have been proud to paint.

'Not much more than a big white pebble on the beach' This thinking aloud of Paul's ties in with the rest of the mysticism in this chapter.

Miriam made me feel . . . and nowhere else Paul can use appropriately earthy language at times.

I just go like a leaf down the wind An image which aptly expresses his lack of rational volition.

Morel had not much time This is the first time in the novel that Paul is called by his surname – and it may well indicate the author's mood when he has just described Paul's selfish reactions to Clara.

He felt his whole body unsheath itself like a claw The image indicates the primitive nature of the reaction.

He shivered with pleasure The sadistic streak in human nature, here conveyed with commendable and telling economy.

He was a pure instinct, without reason or feeling One gets the impression that in a way Lawrence approves of this.

like a screw that is gradually increasing in pressure An image from domestic observation or industry.

Tha has landed then? You've come back, I see.

trapse Journey.

The long grey hair floated . . . of the chimney Almost certainly a piece of unobtrusive symbolism which anticipates his mother's death.

gently, tenderly, as if she were a lover Once again we recur to the title of the novel.

behint-hand Lazy in doing things.

Chapter 14 The Release

Dr Ansell gives Paul the news that Baxter Dawes is in the fever hospital in Sheffield. He has no will to get better, and Paul goes to visit him. At first there is no connection between them, for Dawes is sulking, and Paul talks of his mother's illness. He leaves Dawes some money, and tells Clara the next day that her husband has typhoid. She is very upset, and tells Paul how much more real Dawes' love for her was than his own. Paul is somewhat humiliated.

Mrs Morel's condition gradually worsens, but it is a lingering death, and Annie and Paul spend many anguished hours. In the end Paul adds some extra grains of morphia in her milk, and midway through the morning she dies. Paul is at first overcome, but recovers and continues to visit Dawes. Eventually he persuades Clara to go back to her husband and, leaving them together, goes off on his own to meet his father. The latter has become even more pathetic, sentimentalizing his wife's death.

the elemental man in each had met Lawrence sets great store by this — in fact it involves recognition of each other and a kind of respect.

'She's going like wax' Here Paul means that she is melting fast, getting smaller. This is poignantly expressed later when there is a constant emphasis on the fact that she resembles a girl, both before and after her death.

She wanted now to be self-sacrificial . . . She wanted to do penance Strangely, one can imagine Miriam feeling the same, doing the same, and having the same images used about her.

the tangled sunflowers dying Their death perhaps symbolic of her own.

she looked like a girl The first of these images. They are poignant and moving, as this almost implies that a 'young' person is dying; yet Mrs Morel's youth died long ago. Even her husband notices, when he dares to look at her, this apparent girlhood in his wife.

like a girl's – warm, laughing with tender love As the end draws near, mother and son are virtually lovers, so much so that Paul rejects Clara or goes to her merely for physical relief for his suffering.

both afraid of the veils that were ripping between them An image used again, and conveying that death, the unknown, is near, and also that they are beginning to show their 'elemental' feelings for one another.

her body felt like ash A vivid, expressive image, which indicates how completely Mrs Morel has fallen away.

It is the living I want, not the dead Mrs Morel's words are a poignant reminder of her own 'I should have watched the living, not the dead' when Paul was taken ill shortly after William's death (6,175).

the black clouds were like a low ceiling A vivid image, again almost symbolic of the death that is to come in the small room.

they all laughed together and shook with laughter This is a reaction typical of people under stress.

among her bitterness was a feeling of relief i.e. because they are able to release their suffering in the way mentioned immediately above.

A smoky red sunset came on slowly, painfully, lingering Paul associates this with his mother's lingering, and immediately thinks that she will die.

like dark bubbles in her face An economical, vivid simile.

snugged Comfortable, tucked up.

She lay like a maiden asleep . . . She lay like a girl asleep and dreaming of her love This is seen through Paul's eyes, and is tinged with the idealization of the dead woman; but the image also suggests a return to innocence and peace in death.

And she looked like his young wife again Morel has not dared to look at her during the illness. This strange effect which death produces worries him.

For the real tragedy went on in Morel in spite of himself The meaning is not immediately clear, but what Lawrence is saying is that Morel's fatal weakness of character – his inability to accept responsibility, his need to feel sorry for himself, his self-indulgence – all these continue as before.

nuit blanche A sleepless night (Fr).

the tear in the veil See note above, p.65.

Chapter 15 Derelict

In this moving, short chapter of the novel, Paul finds himself alone. He has, so to speak, willed Clara back to Baxter Dawes, and his father goes to live with a family of old friends. Paul finds concentration especially difficult, is unable to paint, and loses himself in his work. He also goes to pubs quite a lot, but has spells of vacancy, and leads two lives, one superficial, outwardly conforming, and the other a full inner life which often verges on insanity. At times he longs to die and join his mother; at others he realizes that she lives on in him.

He has periods of blank depression in which he does not know who he is or what he is doing; in a sense Paul has lost contact with life, lost the power of reasoning about the relationship of things and people. In his really bad moments he talks to his mother; he grows thin, and is afraid to look at himself in the mirror. Then one Sunday he goes to church and sees Miriam. He snatches at her to see if she can save him from his own self-misery. One evening together is enough to demonstrate their essential incompatibility. Miriam at one stage, perhaps, could have taken him, but she is unable to bring herself to do so. If Paul had made the decision to marry her she would have accepted it, but she is unable to make a decision herself. Miriam leaves, convinced that one day Paul will return to her. Paul considers the vastness of the night, his mother and his agony, and then turns towards the city.

crawling about on the mud of it The image is degrading to Morel.
The swift hop of the paper reminded him she was gone A small thing like this can bring us back from a dream-world to reality.
They were there in their places. But where was he himself? The failure of reasoning power, the inability to see the relationship between things, which is one of the signs of the onset of insanity, in this case temporary delusion.
There was something between him and them It is the deep grief which makes him unable to have a normal relationship for the time being.
The church was like a great lantern suspended A vivid image.
And I should die there smothered Paul understands Miriam's possessiveness and, poignantly, his own inability to give himself completely – the self-failure which he had once confessed to his mother.
She could easily sacrifice herself The only possible image for Miriam.
like the toll of a bell Again a symbolical image – it signifies the death of their relationship.
It was like him to have those flowers Flowers are used symbolically throughout the novel, and Miriam thinks gaudy flowers a reflection on the character of the person who has them.
Little stars shone high up . . . He walked towards the faintly

humming, glowing town, quickly The ending is perhaps the finest piece of writing in the novel. Briefly Paul, contemplating vast space, realizes his own smallness, and also that space is more important than time. He is always to be bound to his mother in soul and spirit, though the ache for her is made worse by this contemplation of the universe. The ending is enigmatic; he turns back towards the town, for there is a need for people if he is not to commit suicide. One wonders even if he is going to Miriam – or perhaps just to carry on in the same old way.

Revision questions on Chapters 13–15

1 Do you find the public house incident between Paul and Baxter Dawes realistic? Give reasons for your answer.

2 Contrast the attitude of Paul and Clara towards their love.

3 Try to give an account of Paul's feelings for his mother at this time.

4 Describe the reactions of (a) Paul and (b) Baxter at the time of their fight.

5 Explain Paul's reactions to the news that his mother is seriously ill.

6 Why do you think Paul goes to visit Baxter Dawes in hospital?

7 Try to define Clara's attitude towards her husband.

8 Do you feel more sympathy for (a) Paul or (b) Mrs Morel during her illness? Give reasons for your answer.

9 Explain how Paul effects the reconciliation between Baxter and Clara.

10 What does Paul feel *initially* after his mother's death?

11 Describe Paul's state of mind as he begins to miss his mother.

12 Why does Paul go to see Miriam again?

13 What is responsible for the failure between Paul and Miriam?

14 Is the ending of the novel optimistic, pessimistic, or neither? Give reasons for your answer.

15 Examine two or three of the stylistic devices used by Lawrence in the final chapter.

Characters

Paul

He was usually active and interested, but sometimes he would have fits of depression

We know that *Sons and Lovers* is essentially an autobiographical novel, and that Paul Morel has many of his author's characteristics in him. He is the pivot around which the whole action of the story moves. From birth Paul is somehow different from his brothers and sister, and perhaps this is exemplified by the baby's action when his mother holds him up towards the 'crimson, throbbing sun', for he lifts up his fist, and his mother is ashamed of 'her impulse to give him back again whence he came'. She decides to call him Paul, and although she does not know why at the time we can guess the reason: Mrs Morel is reacting against the sensual, irresponsible nature of her husband, and subconsciously recurring to the influence of her father, George Coppard, 'who drew near in sympathy to only one man, the Apostle Paul ... he was very different from the miner'. In fact Paul acquires the nickname 'Postle', an ironic reference to the origins of his own name and perhaps also to his character.

Paul's 'difference' in childhood is always stressed, and presages his later sensitivity. Mrs Morel feels that, as a baby, he is trying 'to understand something that was pain'. This draws him very closely to his mother, and in addition he is a sickly and delicate child who constantly requires nursing and care. Thus the way for his later intimacy with his mother, which comes poignantly after the death of William, is prepared. Paul's childhood is laced with incidents which show his possessive love of his mother and hers for him – his sensitivity, his artistic tendencies, his withdrawn and timid nature, and that morbid tendency which he is to indulge so completely after his mother's death.

Paul enjoys helping his mother in the home, and even when he is a young man courting Miriam the turning of the home-made bread is his responsibility. As a child he resents his father, and after his mother's death he despises Morel's sentimentalizing of his wife. So subject is he in childhood to his mother's influence that Paul accepts her standards of judgement in everything. Thus when he has to collect his father's money he notices that Mr Braithwaite and Mr Winterbottom are 'common', and this reflects his incipient ambition to be accepted into the middle-class (which William has succeeded in doing), an ambition fostered by Mrs Morel.

Paul learns French, and constantly strives for culture; he obtains a job which involves long hours and travelling, but it is a respectable job and, as the years go by, he rises to a position of responsibility. His relationship with his mother has given him a certain effeminacy, though at the same time it assures him an insight into the ways of women; consequently Paul gets on well with the girls in the workroom at Jordan's. He is friendly and considerate to them; with Polly, the overseer, he forms the kind of friendship that he needs to give him confidence and security in his work. He takes his lunch to her regularly, and she warms it up for him. With Fanny, the hunchback, Paul is cheerful, and on one occasion he takes down her hair for her – he always has the artist's awareness of human beauty.

There are certain crises in Paul's life, and at each of these his health fails him. The first is the sudden death of William. There is hardly a more poignant moment in *Sons and Lovers* than when Mr and Mrs Morel return from London.

Saturday night, as Paul was turning the corner, coming home from Keston, he saw his mother and father, who had come to Sethley Bridge Station. They were walking in silence in the dark, tired, straggling apart. The boy waited.
'Mother!' he said, in the darkness.
Mrs Morel's small figure seemed not to observe. He spoke again.
'Paul!' she said, uninterestedly.
She let him kiss her, but she seemed unaware of him. (6,171)

Paul feels rejected by the only person he cares for, and the result is pneumonia, a dangerous illness, and the re-establishment of closeness with his mother. From now on the obsessive quality of their love for each other becomes more apparent. Throughout Paul's affair (though that is hardly the correct word) with Miriam, the shadow of Mrs Morel casts itself over his actions and reactions. The mother's ill-concealed dislike of Miriam, a domestic situation which is still likely to flare into terrible scenes, his own physical frustration because of Miriam's physical inadequacy, all these drive Paul closer to his mother. One evening there is a bitter exchange between them, and Paul discovers something which he is never likely to put into the background of his mind again: 'Instinctively he realized that he was life to her. And, after all, she was the chief thing to him, the only supreme thing' (8,261).

The resultant scene underlines the stranglehold that each has on the other emotionally; yet neither is aware of the danger inherent in it, neither feels that such love is corrosive to the spirit and independence of the individual. Paul in fact cannot bear to see his mother break down, as the following extract shows:

'I can't bear it. I could let another woman – but not her. She'd leave me no room, not a bit of room –'

And immediately he hated Miriam bitterly.

'And I've never – you know, Paul – I've never had a husband – not really –'

He stroked his mother's hair, and his mouth was on her throat.

'And she exults so in taking you from me – she's not like ordinary girls.'

'Well, I don't love her, mother,' he murmured, bowing his head and hiding his eyes on her shoulder in misery. His mother kissed him a long, fervent kiss.

'My boy!' she said, in a voice trembling with passionate love.

Without knowing, he gently stroked her face. (8,261–2)

The whole passage is important because of its subtle indications of the pressures on Paul, pressures which are intensified immediately, for following the scene with his drunken father, it is obvious to Paul that his mother is ill. He accepts what Lawrence calls 'the bitter peace of resignation', and consequently finds the strength – and the cruelty – to reject Miriam.

Even in this rejection, though, another facet of his character is displayed. Paul is fundamentally insecure, uncertain of his function in life, and this means that it is impossible for him to make a clean break. Even after his mother's death he returns to Miriam on one occasion, seeking marriage as the basis of security. The title of the chapter in which his reactions are described, 'Derelict', is a sufficiently poignant indication of his lost state when the 'supreme thing' has gone from his life. This final crisis finds Paul mentally and emotionally unhinged; he lives in a delirium of the spirit which ultimately drives him to Miriam, so great is his need for security and reassurance.

There is a consistent development of Paul's character over the course of the novel; when his mother withdraws her love from him, he becomes physically ill, and when she dies he becomes emotionally scarred. His own life, in both instances, is in the balance.

Paul, like his creator, lives intensely. He has a great capacity for tenderness, yet this is sharply balanced against his need to hurt and be hurt. He hurts Miriam out of the frustration she breeds in him, he hurts Clara by the withholding of himself, his real self, in their most intimate moments. Perhaps the strangest instance of his need to be hurt is seen in his relationship with Baxter Dawes. Paul is always aware of Dawes; his initial dislike of him (Dawes is common and coarse, by Paul's standards) changes to an attitude in which Paul's own sense of justice is linked with a mystical communion with the man he feels he has wronged. The scene at Jordan's which leads to Dawes being summoned for assault by old Mr Jordan shows Paul in his teasing, tormenting mood: Dawes is driven to fury by his self-command. But, characteristically, Paul's testimony in court is devoid of hypocrisy: 'Dawes took occasion to insult Mrs Dawes and me because I accompanied her to the theatre one evening; then I threw some beer at him, and he wanted his revenge' (13,425).

Paul knows that Dawes will attack him if possible and indeed goes out of his way to be beaten up by Dawes. One can conclude only that Paul's sense of guilt over Clara makes this necessary to him, and that the physical suffering in some way compensates for the wrong he feels he has done her husband. But this is not the end. Paul visits the sick Baxter in Sheffield, and is instrumental in bringing Clara and Baxter together again. He tells Clara of Dawes' suffering; he tells Dawes that Clara is tired of him (Paul). This could be put down to a genuine desire to see them reconciled, but it is more likely that Paul, unable to have a complete relationship with a woman while his mother, albeit tenuously, still lives, seeks to rid himself of the encumbrance of Clara. It is thus a reflex of Paul's incapacity for full living, an aspect of emotional immaturity.

Although at first sight Paul would appear to have inherited little from his father, he has something of his sensual nature. Paul is powerfully aware, after his experience with Miriam, of the importance of sexual fulfilment and, strangely, speaks of his parents as having known such fulfilment early in their love. He achieves physical harmony with Clara, and for a time is satisfied, but of course the omnipresence of his mother in his mind makes it impossible for him to be happy for long. He has, too, an artistic awareness of feminine beauty which lifts him into a different sphere of experience from that of his father. Perhaps this is best shown in his reaction to Miriam: 'She had the most beautiful body he had ever imagined. He stood unable to move or speak, looking at her, his face half smiling with wonder' (11,353).

We remember his sketches of Clara's beautiful arms, but his capacity for imaginative experience and 'wonder', to use Lawrence's word, is comprehensive. Later in the same chapter we are told that the 'beauty of the night made him want to shout', and immediately afterwards he determines to break finally with Miriam. Sexual awareness and emotional stress or tension always heighten Paul's imaginative responses. The intensity of his nature leads him often to mystical speculation of such occasions. Paul is far from ordinary, and his realization of the complexity of existence, of the unanswered questions about the universe and about man, gives him a strong individuality.

Owing to his relationship with his mother, Paul tends to be incurably romantic, often chivalrous. He is naturally deferential to women, and the workgirls at Jordan's worship him. They certainly spoil him; they make a present of a box of oil-paints on his twenty-third birthday. One manifestation of his romanticism is his decking his mother, Miriam and Clara with sprays of flowers; another is his referring to Clara as 'the Queen of Sheba'; or his attempts to protect Miriam from criticism at the hands of his mother or her brothers.

However, perhaps the most romantic aspect of Paul's character is shown in his relationship with his mother; he constantly refers to her as 'Little' (perhaps a convenient abbreviation of 'My little one'), and he treats her as his 'girl' when he takes her out in Nottingham, Lincoln, or on holiday in Mablethorpe. He is proud of her, tells her to look 'ikey', to show off, and says at one stage: 'You forget I'm a fellow taking his girl for an outing.' As she is dying he frequently stresses the fact that she looks like a girl. This romantic conception is twofold in its effects. Firstly, it shows that for all his knowledge Paul is very naive, seeing no injury to himself or his life in this devotion to his mother. Secondly, the frustration of his having an old and ailing mother when he wants to love a young and healthy one, underlines the pathetic nature of his fixation. In Lincoln she has to rest because, she says, her heart 'is a bit old'. Paul's reaction is powerfully described: 'He did not answer, but looked at her. Again his heart was crushed in a hot grip. He wanted to cry, he wanted to smash things in fury' (9,295).

As Mrs Morel's illness becomes worse this bitterness gives way to resignation; then, immediately after her death, to illusion: 'She was young again ... She would wake up. She would lift her eyelids. She was with him still. He bent and kissed her passionately' (14,485–6). But this in turn is supplanted by uncertainty, the feeling strong upon him that it might be better to die.

So far this examination of the character of Paul has stressed the fact that he lives intensely, in suffering and in love. Though highly sensitive, Paul has his relaxed moments, even as a child. There are occasions when he takes a pride in helping his father and, of course, there is the constant domestic round with his mother. When he goes to work at Jordan's, after the initial diffidence in his nature has been overcome, he finds simple happiness in talking and singing with the girls, and on one occasion in his own home – in an exchange with Beatrice – he reveals a very sharp sense of humour and, more, a sense of fun.

With Edgar, Miriam's brother, Paul enjoys a good friendship with plenty of physical activity as well. Although he is not a fighter, Paul does not heed the warnings of Clara about Dawes and, when he is attacked, rather gives himself up to the primitive experience of hitting back and trying to injure.

Among other things, Lawrence believed that industrialism and mechanization had caused people to lose the capacity for living; let it be said that the salient characteristic of Paul is that he really *lives*. Paul is passionately devoted to his home – despite the presence of the erring father – to his mother, brothers and sister, to the beauties of nature which he is to paint, to literature. Later, he feels a strong spiritual affinity with Miriam (although he cannot sustain it), a passionate sexual attraction to Clara, and all the time his mind is searching, questioning his life, his responses to life, his love and his grief.

To read *Sons and Lovers* is to live with Paul Morel, to share his experiences, warm or bitter, sad or frustrating. Characterization which has its roots in autobiographical actuality often bears the impress of abiding truth; it is so with Paul. He is far from perfect – many of his actions, particularly with Clara and Miriam, are undertaken in blind selfishness – but he is never less than human. A list of character 'points' would demonstrate little, for he has the malleable, vibrant reflexes which are felt rather than recorded.

Mrs Morel

Nothing is as bad as a marriage that's a hopeless failure

The quotation above is the key to the character of Mrs Morel. In most great novels the verisimilitude created by the author is so convincing that the reader finds himself thinking about the *alternative* lives the characters might have led. Mrs Morel is so real that we are forced into this kind of speculation, and in view of her qualities it is far from idle. Gertrude Morel, née Coppard, is a woman of dauntless and daunting character; married to a man who is weak and irresponsible, she devotes herself to the bringing-up of her children; economic circumstances, generally traceable to Morel's drinking habits, sometimes force self-denial upon her and the children. But she never denies them her love and protection. What might she have been had she married differently?

Mrs Morel likes to discuss philosophy and religion with Mr Heaton, the local congregational clergyman, and she joins the Women's Guild and sits at home preparing papers to read to them, much to the interest of her children. The term 'daunting' was used above to indicate the power of her personality – she is considered superior by her neighbours, she can quell her husband by sheer strength of character (except when he is too drunk to know what he is doing), she is one too many for Miriam on all occasions, and Clara goes in some awe of her. Once she puts a waitress in her place, to Paul's embarrassment (5,123).

Mrs Morel's environment, the conditions of near poverty, force her towards snobbery. Frustrated by her own life, she comes to want for her children what she herself can never have, has never had, in her own life. Her intense ambition is in effect an extension of herself, a vicarious participation in the lives she has made:

Now she had two sons in the world. She could think of two places, great centres of industry, and feel that she had put a man into each of them, that these men would work out what *she* wanted; they were derived from her, they were of her, and their works also would be hers. (5,127–8)

Initially William, the eldest, is the focus of her attention and efforts; eventually he obtains a position in London with a shipping firm, returning home at Christmas and holidays. As he becomes infatuated with 'Gyp', so Mrs Morel sees her own hopes of happiness for him diminish; she refuses to go to bed until they have retired, deplores William's financing of his fiancée, and asserts her own standards unflinchingly. Then comes the telegram which takes Mrs Morel to London and her dying son; with typical courage she does what she has to do. Even the telegram she sends to her husband has the strength, the brevity, of her taut nature: 'William died last night. Let father come, bring money' (6,169).

All the enforced economy, the habitual repression of feelings which had been her lot in life, are condensed into those few words. Only the serious illness of Paul, as his aunt remarked, saved Mrs Morel herself; in her own words, 'I should have watched the living, not the dead.' Paul becomes the living for whom she herself now lives.

In Part 2 of the novel Mrs Morel's reactions to Paul's affairs with Miriam and Clara are described; she appears fitfully before the chapter called 'Release', which deals with the final stages of her illness and subsequent death. Before dealing with Mrs Morel in Part 2, it might be as well to review briefly the importance of her role in Part 1. This early section of *Sons and Lovers* is a study of family life, and everything turns on the reactions of the mother. Firstly we are shown Mrs Morel deluded, about her husband and about her home, and this is followed by her reactions to the degradation of the intimacy she is forced to endure. But there is never any question of her breaking down under the pressure. On one occasion Morel locks her out after he has come home drunk, and the spirit of the woman is powerfully conveyed as she walks in the garden:

Mrs Morel, seared with passion, shivered to find herself out there in a great white light, that fell cold on her, and gave a shock to her inflamed soul. She stood for a few moments helplessly staring at the glistening great rhubarb leaves near the door. Then she got the air into her breast. She walked down the garden path, trembling in every limb, while the child boiled within her. (1,34)

Mrs Morel protects William from her husband after a neighbour's complaint, and with a terrible and conscious fixity of purpose she shuts Morel out of the family life, not by ignoring him (in fact when Paul wins a prize she insists on his telling his father), but by inflexibly pursuing the right course for her children. It must be added that although we are told of her gay moments with Paul (after he has got the job at Jordan's, for example), conditions have ensured that any sense of humour she might possess has been stifled.

Mrs Morel is most vividly conceived in this first part of the novel. We remember particular instances, for example when Paul presents her with a spray of blackberries: '"Pretty!" she said, in a curious tone, of a woman accepting a lovetoken' (4,88). We are made aware this early of her love relationship with her sons which is so ironically foreshadowed in the title of the novel. Mrs Morel is uncompromising to any girl of William's who dares to come calling for him, and yet, strangely enough, she treats 'Gyp' with compassion, although the girl is of a different social class and condescends to the family.

While she talks with William she observes his treatment of 'Gyp', and perhaps she sees in their strife some equivalent to her own struggle with Morel. She may even see in William, for Mrs Morel possesses a natural wisdom, some flaw, some aspect of his father (William blames 'Gyp' when things go wrong, just as Morel blames her) which detracts from his character. One particular facet of her own character must be given due weight, and this is her loyalty to her husband. She goes to Nottingham to see him when he is badly injured, nurses him when he is unwell at home; the outside world knows little or nothing of her sufferings.

There are moments too, when one feels that Mrs Morel's love for her husband is not completely dead, though she quickly represses any manifestation of affection towards him. Certainly she never ceases to despise herself for having made the initial error of loving him. Lawrence makes two brief statements which sum up the position of Mrs Morel in this first part of the novel. The first is: 'She was a woman who waited for her children to grow up.' The second poignantly underlines her personal deprivation, social rather than matrimonial, as Paul is being interviewed by Mr Jordan. We are told that she 'sat quiet and with that peculiar shut-off look of the poor who have to depend on the favour of others'. Narrow-minded to the point of being puritanical, jealous, scrupulous, practical, a woman with physical reserves, emotional strength and considerable mental powers, Mrs Morel never fails to hold the reader's attention as she fights the good fight to rear her family.

In Part 2 we are soon aware, though nothing is said for some time, of her impending illness. As Paul becomes obsessed with Miriam, Mrs Morel is shut-off until, at the critical moment in a confrontation between Paul and his father, she faints, and Paul realizes that she is ill. Mrs Morel, however, is adept at hiding the serious truth; she allows herself to be provided with a maid, and she wins her son back from Miriam in an almost hysterical outburst in which she acknowledges that she has never really had a husband. This is consummate artistry on Lawrence's part, for Mrs Morel rarely gives way to emotion. She delights in Paul's modest success as a painter, secretly nursing her pride in him; but she has to sit at home while Paul teaches Miriam, or communes spiritually with her, or makes love to Clara.

Mrs Morel has her wish – of uninterrupted possession of him – for a while after he has been beaten by Baxter Dawes. Although she has an 'attack' while he staggers home, she recovers to nurse him, advising him, 'And now I should have done with them all.' He follows this advice in that he is never the same again to Clara, and succeeds in getting her to go back to Dawes. Paul has a brief holiday himself, and goes to his sister Annie's on his return, to find that his mother's disease is far advanced. Suffering greatly, in pain for much of her waning life, Mrs Morel, with characteristic courage and understanding, tries to alleviate Paul's anguish on her account by underplaying her own agony.

With an exquisite and moving truth Lawrence writes of her increased sharpness and her forced gaiety, of her silent rejection of her husband, and seldom in the whole span of the novel are we made more aware of the autobiographical content. Mrs Morel clings obstinately to life, as obstinately as she lived it, but the focus shifts from her to the watcher, Paul. There are many terrible death scenes in fiction, but few are as powerfully immediate as that of Mrs Morel when Annie and Paul, moved to desire what they have feared for so long, hasten their mother's death with an extra dose of morphia. She dies idealized by Paul – he sees at times her death as a dream, his mother as a girl, a princess in a legend – but the moment of truth finds him as it found her with William: 'When he took his face up from his warm, dead mother he went straight downstairs and began blacking his boots' (14,484). In that simple action we see the impress of Mrs Morel, and know that, as she wished, she did indeed live on in Paul.

Walter Morel

He always ran away from the battle with himself

On a superficial reading Morel appears to be the character who fails to awake any sympathy. For the first three chapters of the novel he commands as much attention as his wife, but whereas she invites sympathy he engenders an active repugnance. Yet we can see, particularly from the short, retrospective sequence which describes their courtship, how Gertrude Coppard was attracted to him. Morel worked in the pits from childhood, yet he is capable of deferential behaviour, is naturally charming and virile, and has a certain presence. Moreover he is free from the inhibitions of polite society, and this gives him an immediacy of appeal denied to the conventional.

At first he and his young wife are happy; gradually a moral scar in the character of Morel is uncovered which spreads as the years pass. He misleads his wife about the furniture and their home; he is known to be a drinker and something of a ladies' man, though she is the last to find out. As the children arrive, so Morel turns away from his responsibilities, calculating the weekly budget after he has set aside so much for drink. Over the course of his life he changes his pubs but not his habits; sometimes he helps in a pub, sometimes he arrives home in a high good humour, sometimes he arrives truculent, dangerous, violent. The children tremble at his temper and threats, and later come to despise him.

Morel has no ambition, keeps to the company of drinking companions outside his home, and his domestic habits, sometimes deliberately over-acted, are calculated to offend the refined or the sensitive. Consider, for example, his fierce and obdurate assertiveness to Mr Heaton, the congregational clergyman he finds taking tea with his wife, his bullying shouts when the children make too much noise, his physical assaults on his wife when he is the worse for drink; and he never loses sight of the class war between himself and his wife, an awareness which they both share, so that there is a bitter irony in his calling her 'a nasty little bitch', and in her referring to him as 'My lord'.

Though Morel backslides from the economic and moral responsibilities of life, he has some qualities which can only be described as lovable. Consider his cobbling or his making of fuses, when the children are delighted to help him, or his telling of stories about the pit; consider, too, his tenderness when Paul is ill, a tenderness that is strangely moving and isolated if one thinks of the fierce love of the children for their mother to the exclusion of their father.

One remembers too Morel's excitement when William comes home for the first time at Christmas, his silent reception of the news that William is dead, and his refusal to walk past the office where his son had worked, or to go near the cemetery where he was buried. And at one of Paul's moments of great triumph, when he wins first prize at an exhibition at Nottingham castle, it is Morel's reaction which is a terrible reminder of the fact that he recurs to the family tragedy beneath the daily routine:

His black arm, with the hand all gnarled with work, lay on the table. His wife pretended not to see him rub the back of his hand across his eyes, nor the smear in the coal-dust on his black face.
    'Yes, an' that other lad 'ud 'a done as much if they hadna ha' killed 'im,' he said quietly. (10,311)

What is noticeable, too, in Lawrence's presentation, is the convincing way he makes Morel gradually age. Apart from a drunken brush with Paul, Morel is rarely present in the second part of the novel, and it is almost as if Lawrence, like the Morel family, has rejected him. However, the spaced moments have their own telling effect; we begin to ask ourselves what has happened to the husband who was so positive, usually for evil, in the earlier history of the family. On one occasion we find him washing before the share out with his mates from the pit, and again there is this direct insight into his feelings:

Morel watched her shyly. He saw again the passion she had had for him. It blazed upon her for a moment. He was shy, rather scared, and humble. Yet again he felt his old glow. And then immediately he felt the ruin he had made during these years. He wanted to bustle about, to run away from it. (8,243)

And he does. But the pathetic, human quality adheres to him; he is morally frail, but he is not beyond our sympathy. This is given a considered stress when Mrs Morel is taken seriously ill and he comes to see her. We are told that he looked 'Helpless, and as if nobody owned him', and once again he wishes to run away from the situation. Mrs Morel returns to her home: 'Morel wanted to carry her indoors, but he was too old. Arthur took her as if she were a child' (13,460).

The father has been finally and completely eclipsed, and he

now appears only on the fringes of the action. We are reminded that he is living in the same house as the dying woman only by a very occasional mention. These mentions are all in character; as death approaches, 'Morel, silent and frightened, obliterated himself. Sometimes he would go into the sick-room and look at her. Then he backed out, bewildered' (14,478).

On the day of her death he looks at her in fear; but that death is not only her release, it is a release for them all. Morel can now take refuge in talking sentimentally of his wife to her relations and in the bars with his friends. Still there eats into him the memory of their life together, and there is a terrible moment when his loneliness almost unmans him:

His father looked so forlorn. Morel had been a man without fear – simply nothing frightened him. Paul realized with a start that he had been afraid to go to bed, alone in the house with his dead. He was sorry. (14,486)

One need hardly add that the reader is moved to pity too, and again when, somewhat later, he creeps downstairs in the afternoon to tell Paul, 'I *have* been dreaming of thy mother.'

It says much for Lawrence's own compassion – and he has not been overpraised for this – that in the presentation of his father's character there is a wise awareness that it takes two people to make a wrong, particularly a wrong that lasts throughout their lives. His heart is largely with the woman who stands for his mother, but life undoubtedly taught him that a small corner of it belonged to the father who, incapable of self-discipline, was capable of vitality and warmth, kindliness and concern, but without the moral fibre that makes those qualities of surpassing value in many a person.

Miriam

She was ruddy and beautiful. Yet her soul seemed to be intensely supplicating.

Miriam first enters the action of the novel when Paul and his mother go up to Willey Farm to visit Mrs Leivers while Paul is recuperating from his illness. She and Paul are drawn to one another by a love of nature, but the first descriptions of Miriam do not augur well for her future intimacy with Paul:

The girl was romantic in her soul. Everywhere was a Walter Scott heroine being loved by men with helmets or with plumes in their caps. She herself was something of a princess turned into a swine-girl in her own imagination. (7,177)

She is dreamy, impractical, greatly influenced by her mother's religious mysticism ('The mother exalted everything – even a bit of housework – to the plane of a religious trust'), and she is possessive to an intense degree. The latter quality is demonstrated when, 'her voice drenched with love', she makes a great fuss of her youngest brother, Hubert.

Miriam's whole relationship with Paul turns on this need to possess him completely from the spiritual point of view, though not from the physical. Brought up on a farm, Miriam is disgusted by, and recoils from, the fact of birth as a result of animals mating. She is revolted at the thought of human physical intimacy, and this is largely because her mother has made a confidante of her and given her a disproportionate view of the man/woman relationship. Even on an ordinary everyday level she is physically afraid, as she shows in the incident with Paul and the swing.

Her own beauty means little or nothing to her, but one of her responses to living in a house of working, practical men is the wish to acquire learning. This brings her close to Paul, as he agrees to teach her French. Miriam uses what French she acquires to write rhapsodic, personal love-letter essays for Paul, and her intensity frequently annoys him beyond measure. Miriam is virtually incapable of living in a relaxed and ordinary way – she burns the potatoes because her mind is elsewhere – and she adopts a religious attitude towards everything. As Paul tells her, 'You don't learn algebra with your blessed soul. Can't you look at it with your clear simple wits?' (7,194).

Miriam is extremely sensitive, easily wounded by her brothers and, as their intimacy deepens, by Paul. The intensity of her nature, the fact that she takes herself so seriously, means that she alienates people very easily. Mrs Morel has no time for her, Beatrice Wyld mocks her, and in her own family she is ridiculed, so that she constantly pays the price of her own individuality. And Miriam, one senses, is born to suffer, so that she comes to accept it as her burden in life.

With Paul, however, the girl has moments of ecstasy. An indication of her emotional and religious temperature is shown when she wishes to show Paul a certain wild rose-bush:

Miriam was getting very eager and very intense. Her bush might be gone. She might not be able to find it; and she wanted it so much. Almost passionately she wanted to be with him when he stood before the flowers. They were going to have a communion together – something that thrilled her, something holy. He was walking beside her in silence. They were very near to each other. She trembled, and he listened, vaguely anxious. (7,197)

Miriam is singularly unable to conceal her reactions to a situation or a person. She appears to enjoy, in a self-smothering way, being in a position where she is likely to suffer. Thus she introduces Paul to her friend Clara Dawes (it is certainly not a deep friendship) and watches Paul's behaviour, ever-fearful that he may be tempted to forsake her. Her own interpretation of such temptation would be that it would reflect a temporary yielding to Paul's 'lower' nature. There is, also, something akin to deliberately undertaken suffering in the way Miriam calls at the Morels' home when she knows that Clara will be there; her sensitivity does not only note Paul's reactions to Clara, but takes in the important difference which she has feared – namely that Paul's mother will like Clara, whereas she was contemptuous of Miriam.

Lawrence subtly indicates Miriam's incapacity for physical fulfilment by describing her, or having Paul think of her, in terms of religious imagery. We have already referred to the 'communion' which she wanted with Paul, and at the moment of physical yielding there is a more powerful suggestion – 'she lay as if she had given herself up to sacrifice'. Paul had earlier written to her: 'See, you are a nun. I have given you what I would give a holy nun – as a mystic monk to a mystic nun . . . In all our relations no body enters.' But though Miriam is capable of physical renunciation – indeed, can easily do without physical contact – Paul is only human, and the advent of Clara ensures that he will leave Miriam.

The language used to describe Miriam is echoed by Lawrence in many of his letters to Jessie Chambers, the original of his study. The tone throughout is strangely unsympathetic, and the impression we take away is that Miriam does Paul more injury by a combination of characteristics, notably 'soul' possessiveness and physical negation, than does his mother. Yet there are moments of pure pathos when she is described. Consider the terrible human isolation of the following:

Miriam loitered behind, alone. She did not fit in with the others; she could very rarely get into human relations with anyone: so her friend, her companion, her lover, was Nature. She saw the sun declining wanly.

In the dusky, cold hedgerows were some red leaves. She lingered to gather them, tenderly, passionately. The love in her finger-tips caressed the leaves; the passion in her heart came to a glow upon the leaves. (7,205)

In fact Miriam is a fascinating character because she *is* predictable, the pattern of her life has made her what she is and what she will be. She is so uncertain, so ignorant in the ways of the human as distinct from the mystical heart, that she tactlessly urges Paul to make physical love to her when he least wants to because of his suffering over his mother. And when he most wants her – when he comes to her after his mother's death – she is inadequate, unable to give him the physical and emotional understanding that he needs. Miriam is so withdrawn into her own world, so oblivious of the feelings of others unless they relate to her, so unwilling to make decisions or undertake independent actions, that she cannot take part in life without a rhapsodic or mystical identification with what is going on.

Although she and Paul know one another for many years she cannot read his mind or understand his emotions with any degree of certainty, as is shown when he tells her why he is breaking with her. But Miriam's bitterness is soon transmuted into mysticism. She has, however, exercised quite an influence on Paul which is not without good effects; she encourages him to paint, and understands much of what he is trying to achieve in artistic expression. Miriam helps him to discover his thinking self, for although he once says disparagingly that she is always 'jawing' about something, the range of their discussions could only have been intellectually stimulating.

One understands why Paul is drawn towards Miriam – her beauty, meaningless to her but a constant stimulus to him, her mind, questioning and experiencing, and her 'love' for him, all combine to reduce him, and he never really escapes from the trammels of her spirituality. But Paul is of this world and living; Miriam, humourless, serious, heavy, devotional, nun-like, lives in a spiritual self-communion far removed from the normal regions of experience.

Clara

Yet she was perfectly amiable, but indifferent and rather hard

Clara Dawes, separated from her husband Baxter Dawes, is first introduced to Paul by Miriam. She is some six years older than he, is interested in women's rights and speaks at the meetings, and is supposedly contemptuous of men. The first description of her is lavish and full of promise that she is not merely what she appears:

She had scornful grey eyes, a skin like white honey, and a full mouth, with a slightly lifted upper lip that did not know whether it was raised in scorn of all men or out of eagerness to be kissed, but which believed the former. (8,228)

Paul is himself anxious to meet her again, although he does not find her pleasant, and their conversation hinges on Clara's bitterness about the status of women and the menial tasks which they have to do. However, when the three of them go for a walk there is an important episode which does much to explain Clara's attitude; they meet Miss Limb, are aware of her loneliness, and aware also, none more than Clara, of what her love for the horse really covers. This is, as Clara blurts out in an unguarded but revealing moment, her need for a man.

This, too, is Clara's need, and her relationship with Paul contains as its main ingredient their strong sexuality which can only mean consummation or separation. Clara has very much a will of her own, and resists for some time. Having determined to go her own way she does so, but she is vulnerable, and knows it, reacting with 'pitiful, scared grey eyes' when Paul scatters flowers over her. She lives in some fear of being 'caught' by a man again, as she demonstrates when Paul visits her for the first time at her home. Admittedly, Clara has the conventional concern as to whether where she lives is good enough, but the interior – mother and daughter at work, with the mother a strongly vocal character – shows how claustrophobic her existence is: 'She spoke humbly to him. He had surprised her in her drudgery.'

Paul is instrumental in getting her to return to Jordan's where Clara displays the same high-handedness to the other girls which had made her unpopular before. She is aloof, considering herself 'a woman apart' even from the girls of her own class. Like Miriam, she has had some passion for learning, and Paul discovers that she can read French. Even when she comes to Jordan's, however, she gives little away about herself, for we are told that her 'history was open on the surface, but its inner meaning was hidden from everybody'.

Clara's interest in Paul can be gauged from the fact that, when she is left out of the girls' birthday present for him, she quietly buys one for him herself and sends it. Their intimacy deepens. Paul even talks to her of Miriam, but his frustration in that direction really leads him to Clara, for they are each strongly aware of the other physically.

'They had grown very intimate unawares' is the way Lawrence puts it. Clara shows that she is more and more attracted to Paul, and they spend a rapturous afternoon together. Although she still resists, it is obvious that she is deeply in love with him. He spends the night at her home after a visit to the theatre with her, though she had previously denied him after she had visited his mother.

Their love scenes together are impassioned, and are lyrically described. Clara's reactions are not measured in the same detail as Paul's, and when Paul tells her of the incident in which he has thrown beer in Baxter's face, he seems to start a chain association in her: 'Clara was happy, almost sure of him. She felt she had at last got him for herself; and then again came the uncertainty' (13,420). There is every reason for this, for Paul never really gives himself, in fact he is incapable of doing so while his mother is alive. Clara has come to realize this, and although they continue to have moments of sublime happiness – generally physical ones – Clara begins to feel guilty about leaving her husband.

This is heightened when Clara learns from Paul that her husband has been very ill; and before that, after Baxter has beaten Paul, she probably senses on the few occasions she visits Paul that the latter has taken his mother's advice and wants to get all of them out of his system. Here Clara appears to act courageously, though there is a residue of pathos in her character. She tells Paul that she had Baxter more completely than she has had him, and thus becomes the second woman to puncture his ego (Miriam was the first). Moreover, although Clara does not fully understand Paul, she makes it quite clear that Paul does not understand her, that he is incapable of giving himself sufficiently to understand:

'You talk,' she said, 'about the cruelty of women; I wish you knew the cruelty of men in their brute force. They simply don't know that the woman exists.'

'Don't *I*?' he said.

'No,' she answered.

'Don't I know you exist?'

'About *me* you know nothing,' she said bitterly – 'about *me*!'

'Not more than Baxter knew?' he asked.

'Perhaps not as much.'

(13,440)

One cannot help but admire Clara's frankness, the more particularly as this kind of statement is not going to endear her to Paul. Above all else one feels that Clara wants some kind of security, away from her mother, and thus she does not object when Paul manipulates her back to Baxter. In a sense she feels that she has used Baxter ill (there is some rough idea of justice in this, for Paul feels that *he* has misused Baxter), and the result is a reconciliation that exposes a certain type of human acceptance. Clara comes around to a way of thinking about Paul, seeing her husband as more manly because he admits defeat whereas Paul will not. The fact is, she knows now that she can rule Baxter, who is much bowed down, and the last we see of her she is getting some enjoyment from the situation:

She made a moaning noise, lifted her arms, and put them round his neck, drawing him to her. He hid his face on her shoulder, holding her clasped.

'Take me back!' she whispered, ecstatic. 'Take me back, take me back!' And she put her fingers though his fine, thin dark hair, as if she were only semi-conscious. He tightened his grasp on her. (14,497).

Clara is an arresting character, physically attractive, positive, her outward aggressiveness or aloofness concealing a deep-rooted insecurity; but she has fine, understanding moments, and a sure insight into human nature.

Baxter Dawes

He was very evidently on the downward track

Baxter Dawes is an interesting minor character, not in any sense fully developed by Lawrence, though he develops in a different way from what we should expect after our two or three brushes with him. He is coarse-grained, imposing physically, and aggressive, the more so after Clara has left him; even before Paul knows Clara he has disliked Dawes' manner, his uncouthness, and has stared at him, to the latter's fury. Although he has a mistress for a time, Dawes has not ceased to watch his wife, as is apparent when he sees Paul and Clara come out of the theatre. He is a shady character, and there is every indication that he is going to seed. Dawes has three major encounters with Paul before he is taken ill himself. The first is in the pub, where his innuendo about Clara and Paul at the theatre shows his own frustration, coarseness, and a certain ominous, vicious streak; the second is in Thomas Jordan's factory, where he is bewildered by Paul's tactics, and where he ends up by causing Thomas Jordan's fall.

One night as Paul is coming home he is waylaid and attacked by Baxter. The latter is very powerful, but loses his head when Paul nearly strangles him, and kicks Paul, injuring him quite severely as he is lying defenceless on the ground. Yet there is little doubt that he feels something of the bond that Paul feels for him – that their hatred is mingled with a certain kinship despite their disparate physical and mental affiliations.

Paul hears that Baxter has contracted typhoid fever and is in a hospital in Sheffield. Baxter is truculent, but Paul does much for him – getting Clara to visit him, helping to rebuild his confidence and make him fit to enter into life fully once again. In fact by this stage Baxter is pathetic, virtually broken. Clara – and Paul –lift him somewhat. Firstly, Clara 'kneeled to Dawes, and it gave him a subtle pleasure'. Secondly, Paul comes to see him at the end of his convalescence:

The two men, between whom was such a big reserve, seemed faithful to each other. Dawes depended on Morel now. He knew Paul and Clara had practically separated (14,488)

Perhaps this knowledge sustains him. He lets himself be influenced by Paul finally, and a certain smugness returns, the 'triumphant male came up in Dawes' as Paul cleverly steers him back to Clara, for it is the direction in which he really wants to go. Baxter takes Clara back (this is her emphasis – in reality she makes the taking back possible) and we see no more of him. Baxter Dawes is functionally necessary to the plot, but the decent-at-heart humble man that he appears at the end is not entirely convincing.

William

A big, raw-boned man, who looked as if he would go to the world's end if he wanted to

William is the eldest child of the Morel family, and all his mother's ambitions focus on him to begin with. In childhood he and Paul both admire one another and yet are secretly jealous of each other too; William bitterly resents his father and, as Paul is to do later, does everything for his mother. On one occasion there is almost a fight between father and son, and only a determinedly timely intervention from the mother averts it.

William appears born to be successful. He mixes well, is very jolly, he goes dancing, girls find him attractive; ultimately he lands a job in London with a shipping firm. William's first Christmas at home after this is warmly, almost lyrically described – his generosity to his family, their pride in him, his open, vivid personality, the general opinion that he is a real gentleman, all these things fuse into a complete and moving presentation. The aftermath of misery when he has returned to London is also feelingly conveyed.

But William is lured from his studies – he intends to go in for law – by the very ease with which he has succeeded in getting into 'genteel' (and largely irresponsible) society. In particular he pays court to a sophisticated, superficial young woman by the name of Lily Louisa Weston, 'Gyp' as he calls her, and this relationship proves to be a demoralizing one for him. His presents to his family – and much needed money with which he had previously helped – cease, and he brings Miss Weston home. The girl patronizes the family – Annie is virtually a maid to her throughout her stay – and there is overt friction between 'Gyp' and William in front of the family.

Mrs Morel has not seen her son so bitter before, but with that adhesive of consistency which convinces, Lawrence has made William in some manner his father's son. He knows that he is misguided in keeping on with 'Gyp', but William lacks the fundamental willpower to break it off. This he confesses to his mother in some poignant exchanges – he is financially bound to 'Gyp' as she is to him, buys her underclothes and her food, and holds tenaciously to an unspecified moral obligation to her. William ceases to take any interest in things outside 'Gyp', though he continues to abuse her to her face, and gradually declines in health.

His death from pneumonia is a sudden shock, a superb example of Lawrence's economy of treatment to produce a tragic effect. As William predicted, 'Gyp' soon forgets him; his death ensures his mother's ultimate concentration on Paul as the 'be-all and end-all' of her life. Our memory of William is chiefly of the boy, alive and intelligent, devoted to his mother, popular, generous and open-hearted as he comes to young manhood. He dies, Paul lives, and in the younger brother we often catch a glimpse, a reaction, which might have been William's.

Minor characters

Lawrence has two kinds of minor characters, those who are either caricatures or types, and those who come alive in vivid reality at the stroke of his pen.

The two other members of the family are *Annie* and *Arthur*.

Annie is never fully drawn. As a baby she is generally crying, as a child she annoys Morel with her noise. As a young woman she 'goes steady' with Leonard, a very earnest young man; she is devoted to her home, however, and is critical of Paul's relationship with Miriam. Annie first brings home to Paul the fact that his mother is ill (on the evening when Paul's absorption with Miriam leads to the burning of the bread), and she does not spare him her tongue. Later she and Leonard become frustrated at the dragging on of their courtship – Paul at this stage cannot understand why – and after Leonard has seen Mrs Morel they get married, Annie with many tears. But Mrs Morel says at the time, 'A son's my son till he takes him a wife, But my daughter's my daughter the whole of her life.'

This proves true. When Paul returns from his brief holiday in Blackpool he finds his mother ill in Sheffield at Annie's house. Annie claims that had she been at home she would have noticed the advanced stage of her mother's illness. But with characteristic loyalty and love she returns with Mrs Morel and Paul to nurse her mother through the final stages of the disease. As the end approaches, and the pain gets worse, she conspires with Paul to give her mother additional morphia in her bedtime glass of milk. Annie watches over her mother, and is the first to bring the news of her death. Her last glimpse of her – and our last glimpse of Annie – is when she sees the dark corner of William's coffin as Mrs Morel's is lowered into the grave.

Arthur is somewhat similar to his father, and his career and sensuality until he finally settles are strongly reminiscent of Morel's. Admittedly, one cannot see Morel signing on as a soldier, but the physical descriptions of Arthur strongly suggest his father in his youth.

As a baby Arthur is his father's favourite, crowing to the miner when he enters the room. As a young man he no longer gets on with his father, loves his mother, and yet demonstrates that irresponsible flair which characterizes Morel. He likes dancing and is 'a boon companion' when it comes to drinking. The most vivid evocation of Arthur is when Beatrice Wyld and he make love to one another; it is almost as if Lawrence is showing us a love affair in minor key based on sensuality, to contrast with the Paul–Miriam spirituality. The atmosphere of the exchange, redolent of physical passion, stems largely from Arthur's inherent sexuality:

He grew flushed, his eyes were bright, he sang in a manly tenor. Afterwards they sat together on the sofa. He seemed to flaunt his body: she was aware of him so – the strong chest, the sides, the thighs in their close-fitting trousers (9,302)

Arthur surrenders to the impulse of the moment, thoughtlessly, recklessly, and finds himself married. At first he reacts restlessly in an attempt to escape – the baby makes too much noise, he can't get down to work, he grumbles to his mother. But eventually he disciplines himself, and disappears from our view. As Lawrence puts it: 'He had never been very closely inbound into the family. Now he was gone altogether' (10).

Beatrice Wyld, who becomes Arthur's wife, is vividly drawn. We first meet her when she wanders into the Morel house one evening when Paul and Miriam are together. She is a positive personality, full of life and vivacity, though suffering at times from bad health. Beatrice is obviously intelligent, very much intent on getting a man, has a good if tomboyish sense of humour and, judging from her scene with Arthur, a strongly sensual nature. Miriam's untidiness prompts her to a blunt comment: 'You're a positive muck-heap' – and she engages in a verbal and physical flirtation with Paul ('Postle' she calls him) on this first occasion. Beatrice is forward and self-confident, taking one of Paul's cigarettes, and adopting a mockingly superior social manner as she lights it ('Thanks so much, darling').

Beatrice is also practical, using the nutmeg-grater to try and save the remains of the burnt loaves. She flirts with Leonard when he appears with Annie, and when we next meet her we find that she is strongly drawn towards Arthur. Beatrice, like Arthur (and Paul), relapses into dialect at moments of loving; she has a capacity for tomboyish wrestling as the prelude to lovemaking, and Arthur is subjected to the full treatment, including a slapped face. It all ends in the embrace they both want and the permanence of marriage which is her desire.

Mrs Radford, Clara's mother, causes her daughter much suffering. In a sense, Paul also suffers, for the old lady initially frustrates his making love to Clara on the evening after the visit to the theatre. A few touches of dialogue bring Mrs Radford alive. She is a very sharp woman, 'stately, almost martial', is the first description of her. Mrs Radford is blunt to the point of outspokenness and rules Clara in the home. At the same time she is a realist. She tells Paul to smoke if he wants to, adding: 'A house o' women is as dead as a house wi' no fire, to my thinkin'. I'm not a spider as likes a corner to myself. I like a man about, if he's only something to snap at' (10,318).

She sums up Miriam for Paul's benefit ('She'll never be satisfied till she's got wings and can fly over everybody's head'), and tells Paul, after he has suggested it, that Clara would do well to return to Jordan's. Mrs Radford is unequivocally critical of Clara's evening dress, keeps the lovers on tenterhooks by staying up late – she obviously knows that they want to make love to one another – but she is mollified by Paul, although she disapproves of the situation. Eventually she gets Paul off to bed; but she is a knowing woman, and her remarks the next morning are brimming with innuendo.

'Gyp', or *Lily Louisa Weston*, is an interesting miniature, for she is of a different social class from anyone else in the novel. At first she seems merely a caricature of a society-conscious girl dependent on her men friends for presents; but there are two remarkable facets of her presentation which call for comment, and these are

the fact that she is kindly, understandingly treated by Mrs Morel, and that she engages our sympathies despite our initial disapproval of her. The reason for the latter is obvious, for happiness, depth of character, moral orientation, these things will never be for her. 'Gyp' is pathetic, with her false standards and values; she thinks in terms of clothes and the appearance and impression that she is creating all the time. She goes without food for the sake of clothes, and is used to commanding in a small way. However 'Gyp' is conceived in satire rather than in hate; remember her inability to read a book, and her fiancé's bitter explosion at this failure; remember her constantly losing gloves or scarves, and think of the irresponsibility born of a loveless existence. Think of her wish to be confirmed yet again, and one sees that all is show, and that the show hides the void. 'Gyp' has only her beauty, which will fade; she has no integrity, no taste, and is completely incapable of having a conversation which does not deal with frivolous society matters. Mrs Morel sees this, and realizes that she merits more compassion than censure. 'Gyp' never has any answer – tears apart – to the whiplash of William's tongue.

Mrs Leivers has for some time a great influence on Paul, who loves Willey Farm, but her main influence is on Miriam. We are told that she 'exalted everything – even a bit of housework – to the plane of a religious trust'. This is resented by the rest of the family, Miriam apart, and the latter tends to be her mother's confidante. Paul writes long letters to Mrs Leivers when he goes on holiday in Lincolnshire; he is not only 'in love' with Miriam at this early stage, but with the family, who are cut off from the rest of the world. The boys are described only in passing, with the exception of Edgar, and exist merely as a contrast with Miriam, whom they tease. Edgar claims much of Paul's attention, but he appears merely as a healthy, outdoor lad. Agatha, Miriam's sister, exists solely as another point of criticism of Miriam.

Miss Limb is a fine example of Lawrence's ability to bring a person alive in a few words. She almost pleads for the visitors and company which she is denied. The extent of her neurosis is conveyed in a few chosen words – 'smallish, dark, excitable-looking . . . her dark eyes looked wild . . . lonely, haggard-eyed woman' (9); the intensity of her obsession, in fact, creates the atmosphere of sexuality which causes Paul to move away from

Miriam to Clara. One paragraph is sufficient to achieve this. The others watch the man and the horse being approached by Miss Limb:

'Are you home again, my boy!' she said tenderly to the horse, not to the man. The great beast shifted round to her, ducking his head. She smuggled into his mouth the wrinkled yellow apple she had been hiding behind her back, then she kissed him near the eyes. He gave a big sigh of pleasure. She held his head in her arms against her breast. (9,288)

This moment is indelibly inscribed on the reader's consciousness. (Lawrence developed the study to full-length treatment in a long story called *St Mawr*.)

The rest of the characters in *Sons and Lovers* do not merit real investigation. Annie's *Leonard* is a dull stick, self-conscious, hardly registering with the reader. Morel's friend *Jerry* is really done only at caricature level, as is *Mr Pappleworth*, the 'sporty' man for whom Paul works at the beginning. He teaches Paul how to make out orders, chews lozenges, and is really interested in his Yorkshire terrier bitch. Similarly, *Mr Jordan* is too irascible to be real; he reminds one of a Dickensian character in his limitations of language and attitude.

Two of the girls are brought to life though. *Fanny*, the hunch-back, thirty-nine years old and morbidly sensitive about her deformity, gives Paul the birthday present of the paints on behalf of the other girls. One suspects that she is a little in love with him. The other is *Polly*, the overseer who warms Paul's dinner for him every day, and who helps more than anybody to bring him out of himself. She succeeds in getting Paul to talk about himself and his home, and to sing with them. Even the transitory character, appearing for a few lines only, has the suddenly compelling touch of authenticity. The *'mutual friend'* who encourages Dawes to bait Paul in a seemingly disinterested way is such a masterly brush-stroke, as is *the specialist* who, for his eight-guinea fee, visits Mrs Morel, makes his examination, and meticulously deposits the change on the table before taking his departure, having said little and promised less.

The minor characters exhibit Lawrence's range and underline his powers of observation; whether that observation is at depth or merely a cursory glance, the truth and keenness are apparent.

General questions plus questions on related topics for coursework/examinations on other books you may be studying

1 Give an account of the community in Bestwood and account for Mrs Morel's ambitions to see that her children rise above its influence.

Suggested notes for essay answer:

The description of the mining community; the Morel family, the friction between husband and wife after the initial happiness, Mr Morel's social life, the quarrel(s), the relationship between Mrs Morel and her neighbours. The second part of the question would stress Mrs Morel's history, her superior birth, the frustrations of her life with Morel, her focus of existence being her children, her ambitions for them. Quote in support of what you say, and make sure that you include *detail* of Lawrence's social description and his psychological insights.

2 How far does the character of Paul the boy anticipate the character of Paul the man? Refer to specific incidents in support of your views.

3 Do you consider the love of Paul for his mother and hers for him as being abnormal? (You should consider with regard to this Paul's relations with Miriam and with Clara.)

4 Give reasons for believing that Mrs Morel is a brave woman.

5 Estimate the part played by Walter Morel in the novel, indicating clearly whether or not you sympathize with him, and defining the author's attitude towards him.

6 In what way is William (*a*) like his father, and (*b*) like his mother? Refer closely to the text in your answer.

7 Write a character study of (*a*) Annie, and (*b*) Arthur. Do they reflect any of the characteristics of their father and mother?

8 Do you consider that Miriam is unsympathetically portrayed? Give reasons for your answer.

9 Explain fully the grounds of dislike existing between Miriam and Mrs Morel.

10 Does Clara understand Paul? Give reasons for your answer.

11 It has been said that the incidents involving Baxter Dawes are unconvincing. Would you agree with this?

12 Choose any *two minor* characters outside the Morel family and state clearly what they contribute to the action of the novel.

13 'His great merit is his consummate knowledge of the female mind.' Discuss this estimate of Lawrence's achievements in *Sons and Lovers*.

14 Give *two* examples where Lawrence's poetic description has either a symbolic or a mystical association, and demonstrate how that association influences the reader's response to character.

15 Describe *two* or *three* dramatic scenes from the novel which illustrate the author's power to convey atmosphere.

16 'It is a masterly account of working-class life and carries its own social comment.' Do you agree with this estimate of *Sons and Lovers*?

17 Discuss Lawrence's use of dialect in the novel.

18 'The poetry in *Sons and Lovers* is of a higher order than the realism.' Discuss.

19 'It lacks form and is casually written.' Would you agree with this judgement on *Sons and Lovers*?

20 'Nature has never been painted more truly than in *Sons and Lovers*.' Discuss this statement.

21 Give an account from a book you know well of the presentation of conflict between two characters.

22 Write about the importance of the social and geographical setting in your chosen book.

23 Describe a possessive personal relationship in a book you are studying.

24 Write about an unhappy love affair as it is presented in a book you have read.

25 Write a letter to a friend saying whether you find the ending of a book you are studying satisfactory or not.

Further reading

D. H. Lawrence, Anthony Beal (Heinemann Educational Books, 1968)

Dark Sun: A Critical Study of D. H. Lawrence, Graham Hough (Duckworth, 1968, revised 1970)

Not I, But the Wind, Frieda Lawrence (New Portway Reprints, 1973)

The Collected Letters of D. H. Lawrence, Harry T. Moore (Heinemann, 1962)

Priest of Love: The Life of D. H. Lawrence, Harry T. Moore (Heinemann, 1974)